Animals Among Us

Animals Among Us

Living with Suburban Wildlife

by Fran Hodgkins

LINNET BOOKS

North Haven, Connecticut

First published 2000 by Linnet Books,
the children's imprint of The Shoe String Press, Inc.
2 Linsley St., North Haven, Connecticut 06473.

Library of Congress Cataloging-in-Publication Data
Hodgkins, Fran, 1964–
    Animals among us : living with suburban wildlife / by Fran Hodgkins.
      p. cm.
    Includes bibliographical references (p.).
    Summary: Outlines some of the problems caused by the increasing inter-action of suburban dwellers and animals we think of as wild, such as deer, bears, coyotes, and bats, and discusses the need for local strategies to deal with these problems.
    ISBN 0-208-02478-6 (lib. bdg. : alk. paper)
    1. Urban animals—United States—Juvenile literature.   2. Wildlife pests—United States—Juvenile literature. [1. Urban animals.]   I. Title.
QL155 .H58 2000
591.75'6'0973—dc21   00-021416

Designed by Sanna Stanley

Printed in the United States of America

Key to animal tracks: pages i, 64—raccoon; 1—coyote; 7, 105—gray squirrel; 21—cat; 32—opossum; 50—whitetail deer; 78—red fox; 93—cougar. These are used for decorative purposes only.

For my parents

Contents

Acknowledgments

This book, like all books, could not have been created without the help of many people.

First, I want to thank my editor, Diantha Thorpe, for her suggestions and guidance as we fine-tuned first the idea and then the manuscript.

Thanks very much to the people who took the time to answer my many questions: Maureen Austin; Bob Benson of Bat Conservation International; Frank Brehmer; Heather Carskaddan, Stephanie Stowell and Tammy Schwab of the National Wildlife Federation; Paul Curtis and Rich Malecki of Cornell University; Mike Don Carlos of the Minnesota Department of Natural Resources; Bob Engle of Marlboro College; Lee Fitzhugh of the University of California at Davis; Rich Fletcher of the Mule Deer Foundation; Tom French, Susan Langlois and John McDonald of the Massachusetts Department of Fisheries and Wildlife; Pete Gerl of Whitetails Unlimited; Eric Gordon of CIGNA Corporation; John Hadidian of the Humane Society of the United States; Stephanie Hagopian of the Massachusetts Society for the Prevention of Cruelty to Animals; Bill Heinrich of the Peregrine Fund; Gwilym S. Jones of Northeastern University; Stephen Kavenaugh; John

Leslie and Mary de La Vallette; Steve Lewis of the U.S. Fish and Wildlife Service; Candace McCall, D.V.M., of the Centers for Disease Control; Victor Nettles, D.V.M., of the University of Georgia; Simon Perkins of the Massachusetts Audubon Society; Steven Searles; Laura Simon of the Fund for Animals; and Marsha Sovada and Doug Johnson of the Northern Prairie Wildlife Research Center.

Thanks also to the writers and researchers whose works contributed so greatly to this one; a complete list appears in the bibliography.

Special thanks to Bonnie Hearn; Angela Doucot; Beth O'Connell; my daughter Rosie; and, most of all, my husband Winston. Each of them contributed to this book in ways to numerous to mention, and I'm truly in their debt.

Introduction:
Animals and the Suburbs

Can you walk to the supermarket from your house? Can you buy a new pair of sneakers downtown, or do you take a car to the mall? If your family's car was out of commission for a day, could you get around or would you just end up staying home?

If these questions make you realize how much you depend upon cars, you're probably a suburban kid. You, like a growing number of Americans, need a car to get where you need to go. More and more, families are leaving cities—with their traffic congestion and crowded living conditions—and moving to the suburbs.

Suburbs are communities that are not-quite-city and not-quite-country. They usually have libraries, post offices, schools, restaurants, and video stores. Quite a few have shopping malls, too. But most of all, they have houses, because many people have moved there to live while still keeping their jobs in the city.

The suburbs started in the eastern United States during the 1830s and 1840s, when cities were becoming more crowded and polluted. Some city dwellers started looking for a way out—and what they found were the areas surrounding the cities. This land had, in many cases, once been farmland, but when the worn-out soil could no longer produce abundant crops, the farmers moved west.

1

In these spacious areas, each family could have its own property, and live in a house, instead of in an apartment. Children could play in the yard while their mothers worked around the house and their fathers took the railroad into their offices in the city. Homes like these were seen as refuges from the physical and moral ugliness of the cities, and many people believed that country living brought them closer to nature and God. Trees, flowers, and gardens lent their natural beauty to the suburban refuge. The suburbs grew quickly around major cities, including New York, Boston, Cincinnati, Washington D.C., and Philadelphia.

Residents wanted their homes and yards to be things of beauty—they did not want to re-create the city conditions from which they had fled. It didn't take long for them to hit upon an ideal to copy: the great manor houses in England, which were set on acre upon acre of rolling lawns, uninterrupted by fences or walls. This ideal of a broad, unfenced lawn is still the suburban standard in many places today.

Suburbs really began growing after World War II. At that time, the men who had fought overseas came home and started families, but there wasn't enough housing in the cities for them all. In 1947, six million families were living with relatives or friends. Half a million more were living in temporary houses made from Quonset huts—military storage buildings. Everything that could be lived in was pressed into service, including old grain bins in North Dakota and even retired trolley cars in Chicago.

Clearly, all these people needed inexpensive housing. And real estate developers realized they could make quite a bit of money if they could find a way to provide that housing. But the land available in the cities was not enough, and was too expensive.

The developers turned their sights toward the open land outside of the cities and beyond the already established suburbs. This area was dotted with towns and villages, but it hadn't been built up because it was too far removed from the city. At this time, few people drove their cars to work: they depended on the train, trolley, bus, or their own feet to get around, and these outlying areas weren't served by trolley or train. However, when the car became more affordable and more popular, people realized they could live in one place and drive to another to work or to shop.

The suburbs were a hit. They grew rapidly, and that growth hasn't stopped yet. But to create new homes for people, builders disrupted and destroyed the habitats of millions of birds and animals. Some, like the gray squirrel, adapted to the change successfully and took up residence in the new backyards. However, most creatures moved away, into the shrinking natural areas that remained.

It was not the first time that animals had lost out to people.

The United States was once all wild land. Pines and oaks, birches and aspens stretched from the Atlantic seashore to the grasslands of the Midwest, which in turn changed to the Rocky Mountains, the great Southwestern desert, and then the temperate rainforest on the Pacific coast.

Each of these habitats was full of life. Deer. Bear. Wolves. Cougars. Coyotes. Bison. Pronghorns. Bighorn sheep. Mountain goats. Small creatures like beavers, foxes, raccoons, and prairie dogs. Birds of every description, some in flocks numbering in the millions. Early European explorers couldn't believe the richness of the continent and couldn't wait to tell the people back home.

And the Europeans came in droves, beginning in the 1600s. Colonies started in Florida, Virginia, and Massachusetts. Explorers and commercial venturers raced to claim as much of the new continent as possible for their own countries. The native Americans were conquered, killed, or pushed out. Wars broke out throughout the 1700s as England, France, and Spain each tried to wrest control of the New World from the others. And in 1776, the newborn United States declared its independence from England.

The beaver's pelt was the measure of a fortune during the eighteenth and nineteenth centuries. Photo by Lloyd Poissenot, Louisiana Wildlife and Fish Commission, courtesy of the U.S. Fish and Wildlife Service

After the Revolutionary War, Americans expanded their new states westward into the continent's interior. The Louisiana Purchase of 1803 more than doubled the size of the fledgling country. And there were riches to be had: the woodlands produced huge amounts of timber; all the land teemed with creatures that, once caught, killed, and skinned, could bring a hunter or trapper a handsome payday; and, later, gold was discovered in California.

Once creature to fall prey was the beaver. Even before the rage for fashionable beaver hats in the 1830s, the beaver pelt was desired above all others. In 1703, a trapper could get in exchange for a single beaver pelt:

1 shirt

10 pounds of pork

1½ yards of cotton cloth

5 pecks of Indian corn

2 pints of gunpowder

1 pint of shot

2 small axes

2 small hoes

6 combs, and

6 knives.

Quite a lot of goods for just one beaver skin—and that was well before the beaver-hat rage. In the 1830s, when the hat was most popular, trappers almost wiped out the beaver completely. If not for the arrival of the silk top hat on the fashion scene in 1840, the beaver may have become extinct.

What happened to the beaver happened to other animal species as well. Settlers hunted whitetail deer so intensely that a mere half a million remained (down from a peak number of about thirty million) by the start of the twentieth century. "Sportsmen" slaughtered bison by the thousands, taking the hide and tongue and leaving the rest of the animal to rot. Market hunters killed million of birds for their meat and their skins and feathers, which went to decorate ladies' hats.

Americans would have destroyed these precious parts of nature if not for the foresight of a few people, such as the ranchers who protected the few remaining bison on their private lands. By the late nineteenth century, people began to realize that the nation's natural riches were not inexhaustible but rather needed to be protected and preserved. In 1887, Theodore Roosevelt, an avid hunter, banded together with other men, including George Bird Grinnell, to found the Boone and Crockett Club, which worked to preserve large game animals. Grinnell also founded the National Audubon Society. William Brewster founded several bird groups, including the Nuttall Ornithological Club and the American Ornithologists' Union. William Hornaday not only was a leader of the Bison Society (which helped save that animal from extinction), but also was president of the New York Zoological Society, an early leader in conservation. These organizations carry on conservation efforts today, as do dozens of others such as the Nature Conservancy, the National Wildlife Federation, and the Sierra Club.

Now, in some areas of the country, the cycle has come full circle. The animals that were once driven out or killed are moving back in among us. Bats dot our evening skies, deer browse our gardens, and even bears are spotted climbing telephone poles. It's a change that people are struggling to accept. In most cases, they don't want to kill these wild neighbors. But learning to share "our" property is difficult. We like the idea of having these wild animals around, but many of us, when it comes down to it, would rather have them in someone else's backyard.

In the chapters that follow, you'll read about how some species of animals have made a comeback or even first inroads in America's suburbs, and how people are searching for answers to dealing with the animals among us.

1. A Wildlife Tour of Town

Animals are all around us, day and night, even when we don't realize it. Here's what might go on in your town every day. Right under your nose.

"Come on, Amanda! We're going to be late!" With these words, Maureen Davis urges her 12-year-old daughter away from the window, where she had been watching the birds at their backyard feeder. The Davises gather their gear for the day and hurry out the front door. They walk down the wooden steps, and the noise wakes the raccoon who's been living there for several weeks without their knowledge. He yawns and watches them climb into their minivan. They roar away. The raccoon gives himself a good scratch and goes back to sleep. His day-long nap will only be interrupted a few more times, he knows, by the arrival of the mail truck and the Davis family's return home. But there are hours of good naptime between now and then, in the mild weather of late June. Soon, he's sound asleep again.

The songbirds

The birds at the backyard feeder haven't noticed that the Davises have left. They did notice when Maureen Davis refilled the feeder this morning, and they've been busy eating ever since. Competing for landing space on the feeder platform to snap up sunflower seeds and millet are five house sparrows, a song sparrow, two goldfinches, a veery, a half-dozen chickadees, three juncos, a white-crowned sparrow, and a pair of northern cardinals. They hop and shove, each seeking the best feeding spot.

A sudden whir of wings puts all but the tough little house sparrows and the cardinals to flight. The blue jay and her mate take over one side of the feeder. They flap their wings and cry at two other jays perched on the roof top. The jays on the roof, a pair of new arrivals, have been challenging the resident jays for ownership of the backyard trees and bushes for a week and a half now. The conflicts have been loud, full of screaming, flapping wings and dive-bombing attacks. Eventually, one pair will have to leave. But neither pair is ready to give up yet.

Recognizing a bad situation, the sparrows abandon the feeder to wait until it's less crowded. The scarlet cardinal and his dun-colored mate ignore the agitated jays and crack seeds with their thick bills.

The jays' argument makes even less of an impression on the crows and three gray squirrels that are on the ground below the feeder. They're eating the bread and seeds that Maureen Davis puts there, trying to keep these larger creatures away from the feeder. She thinks this method is working, but it really isn't. Now, the crows and squirrels just clean up the ground before making their assault on the feeder, rather than going right for the main source of food.

The hawk

Suddenly, all the activity freezes. Far overhead cruises a red-shouldered hawk. She's not hunting at the moment, but her presence is enough to clear the feeder. Not one of the songbirds remains.

The crows rise into the air, screaming as the hawk lazily circles overhead. Their cries bring other crows, and soon a gang of twelve crows is assembled. They launch themselves into the air toward the hawk, and their screams carry for miles on the quiet morning breeze.

The hawk isn't disturbed at first. But the cries attract more and more crows to the mob, and the hawk realizes this is not a peaceful place to perch. Tilting her wings slightly, she catches the wind and swoops away.

Mission accomplished, the crows swirl around for a few minutes, calling to each other. Gradually, they drift apart.

The hawk, meanwhile, has flown north on a warm breeze. From her vantage point, she can see the whole town spread out below. She cruises over its compact center, over the post office, police station, and old-fashioned town hall.

The hawk has lived in this area for four years now, and she and her mate have successfully raised three families here. They nest in the stand of trees that was left after the shopping mall was built. The trees are a leafy island at the edge of the vast parking lot, which makes spotting intruders easy. It also has good hunting, being convenient to the shoulders and broad median of the interstate highway, which are full of mice and voles. But the hawk favors hunting in the large open playing fields of the high school, where rabbits are abundant. She turns to the west and heads that way now, unnoticed by the early morning rush hour traffic rolling along Main Road to the highway.

As animals move in among us, they face the dangers of modern traffic.
Photo by the author

At the playing fields, the rabbits are nowhere to be seen. Perhaps they heard the crows and thought it best to hide out. Instead, the grass of the playing field is dotted with giant Canada geese. They rip at the grass with their strong black bills, but pause to watch the hawk. They're too big for the hawk to tackle on her own, so she keeps going.

The geese

The goose that's standing on watch flaps his wings at the retreating hawk. For now, his family is safe, from the hawk at least. Feeding time was nearly over anyway; this seems like a good time to end it and head back to the pond. He honks to his mate and their three nearly grown goslings. With a stately waddle, they leave the soft turf of the field. The sidewalks are empty and don't present a problem to the walking geese. The road between the playing field and the pond is another matter, though. The traffic is still roaring along on it, although it's mid-morning. The road is a hazard the geese must face every time they want to graze.

The gander steps off the curb. He is so tall he can look in the windows of passing cars. He flaps his wings again. The goslings join in, too. A driver in a green station wagon notices the birds and stops, flashing his headlights until a driver in the oncoming lane stops too. The traffic pauses, and the geese waddle across to their pond. They pick their way down the bank and glide into the water.

The man in the green station wagon smiles as he stomps on the gas pedal. He's in a rush to get back home, because he forgot some important papers for a meeting in the city. He turns south off Main Road, drives past the elementary school and into the new subdivision called Country Woods Estates. The man pulls into his driveway and runs up the steps and into the house. The papers are right where he left them. In a flash he snatches them up, runs out to the car and backs out of the driveway. Now that the geese are in their pond, he knows he won't be delayed on his way.

The deer

The man was so focused on getting the papers that he did not see the doe standing in the shadows of the rhododendrons at the side of the house. Her large ears swivel as she listens to the car drive away. Sure now that the coast is clear, she steps quickly across the manicured grass over to the roses. These blooms are her personal favorite, and she eats them like M&Ms. Soon the bush is bare of flowers, and she starts eating another. With only a few pauses to listen to rustlings in the garden, the doe eats her fill. The man won't be happy when he gets home and sees what she's done, but she is content.

The doe leaves this garden and walks up the path beside the house, her hooves making soft clicking sounds on the paving stones. The plants out front are prickly junipers, not one of her favorites, so she ignores them and trots across the street toward a verbena bush. She is just about to take a bite when the dog in the house throws himself against the picture window, barking furiously. The doe raises her tail in alarm, whirls, and sprints back the way she had come.

The dog, panting, watches her go. He would love to chase her, but he can't get out. He has to be satisfied with a few more woofs after the now-vanished deer.

The fox

Six blocks away, on an older street that is not part of the subdivision, a red fox pauses to listen to the dog's furious barking. This vixen knows every house in the southern part of town that has a dog or a cat. Dogs can be trouble for her. Cats less so; they aren't a physical threat to the vixen, who's about the same size as they are, but they do catch and kill the mice she hunts. The yard she's in now is ideal—no dog, no cat, and very little attention paid to landscaping. There's an open compost pile, too, which the mice visit to eat the rotten vegetables and peelings tossed on top. Field mice fill this yard, and it's a good hunting spot. There are enough mice here for everybody: fox, cats, and even the screech owl who is now asleep in the broken cupola topping the ramshackle garage.

The vixen pauses beneath the low-hanging branches of a blue spruce. She can tell by the smell that the compost pile hasn't been added to recently. Two mice poke around on it, searching for food.

The vixen chooses her target and leaps into the air, aiming for the mouse on the right with her forepaws. *Foom!* The mouse is hers. As she gulps it down, she looks around for the other one, but it's gone. That's all right. One mouse in the stomach is better than two in the compost pile. The vixen decides to dig a little, looking for anything that might supplement her small meal—an overripe tomato, a stray chicken bone, a half-moldy cucumber.

She's intent on her digging until a strong scent reaches her nose. She lifts her head and sniffs the midday breeze. The scent is coming from the north, so it's time for the vixen to head south. This is a resident she doesn't want to meet.

She trots away quickly before the coyote sees her.

The coyote

The coyote and his mate are the newest arrival to this area, and the smaller creatures—foxes, cats, opossums, and others—quickly learned to give them a wide berth. Although in the wilderness he'd be vulnerable to larger predators like wolves and cougars, in this suburban wilderness he's the top dog.

The coyote strides through the yard and by the compost heap. He pauses to sniff and notes the vixen's passing, but he doesn't pursue her. Easier prey, such as a mouse or a squirrel, or even a bowl of dog food left on a porch, is more on his mind today.

The coyote walks around the front of the house and climbs the steps to the porch. He sniffs around, but there is no food here. He trots back down the steps and up the street. Over the course of his patrol, the coyote will cover the entire town. The traffic along this road doesn't disturb him, and the few drivers who pass take no notice of him—as they whiz by, they think he's just another dog.

The coyote turns left and trots down an embankment into the playground next to the elementary school. From past experience, he knows that this is a good spot to find misplaced lunches. His nose is sharp and leads him to a brown paper bag. He quickly rips through the bag and the plastic wrap and devours the baloney and cheese sandwich inside. For good measure, he eats the package of cookies, too. The noon bell rings at the school; someone inside will soon discover his lunch is missing.

Licking his lips, the coyote trots away from the school, across the playground and up onto the eighth fairway of the country club's golf course. The smell of grapes hangs heavily in the air, although there aren't any vines for miles. The country club sprays the grape smell as a goose repellent. It works: the geese stay on the high school playing field and avoid the golf course.

The coyote isn't bothered by the grape odor, though, and keeps moving. He checks all along the edges of the fairways, snapping at mice and chipmunks. Today they're all too quick for him, but he isn't trying too hard, either; after all, he's already had a sandwich, and the day is just beginning.

A familiar scent reaches his nose and he trots faster. His mate appears over the top of the hill where the putting green is. She's caught a couple of voles in the rough, but is still hungry.

The ducks

Together, the coyotes prick up their ears as they hear a faint *pip-pip-pip*. The sound comes from mallard ducklings. The coyotes knew the mallards had laid their eggs, but didn't realize the eggs had hatched. A duckling would be a nice change from mice, trash, and baloney sandwiches. They follow the stream that cuts through a grove of trees.

On the opposite bank stand the female mallard and seven fuzzy gold-and-brown ducklings. Her mate is already in the water. The coyotes pause. They had hoped to find the ducks on this bank, not the opposite one. Right now, all they can do is stare. The drake mallard sees them and flaps his sturdy wings. The coyotes are not moved by the drake's display and begin looking for a way across the water.

"Hey! You! Git!" On the bank above the ducks a man with a white beard appears, waving his arms and shouting. The coyotes dive into the safe cover of the trees. They'll check the ducks another day.

The man watches the coyotes go and chuckles. "Guess we scared them off, huh?" he says to the ducks. They preen their feathers and ignore him. With a smile, he drops several slices of bread and walks back to his auto repair shop, which backs up onto the stream bank.

The woodchuck

When the man is gone, a brown head with black buttonlike eyes pokes out of a hole. The woodchuck has lived here even longer than the ducks, and is used to the handouts of bread. She lumbers out of her burrow, grabs two slices of bread and takes them back inside to eat them.

This woodchuck's a bit bigger than the average member of her species, tipping the scale at about fourteen pounds. Blame it on that good bread, and the fact that she's active only for six hours during each day. She'll sit in the mouth of the burrow and watch the activity at the auto repair shop, and seek out new shoots of grass. She spends the rest of her time sleeping in the burrow. She's much less active than her cousins the gray squirrels, who are chasing each other around and around the trunk of an old maple tree.

The squirrels

The gray squirrels used to be rare around here, but over the last century their population has exploded. They've learned that areas settled by humans are ideal habitats, better, even, than the great old forests they used to live in before logging wiped them out. The survivors moved into areas where they lived in backyards and in the trees that lined streets. These two capering squirrels are descendants of such migrants.

Life in this town is so good, in fact, that there are more squirrels here than in the forest. Although they have to watch out for cars and cats, the squirrels find plenty of food (thanks to folks like the Davises and their backyard bird feeders), and can often travel for miles through the treetops and across power lines, never setting a paw on the ground.

These two squirrels leave off their chase game and head east, away from the ducks and the woodchuck. They race along the branches out to the very tips and fling themselves into the air, catching the tips of the next tree's branches. Over and over, tree after tree, they travel this way, to the edge of the wetland in the south end of town. Here they have their nest in a dying oak tree. They have picked this oak because the water has risen around its base—not good for the tree, but excellent for the squirrels, because any potential predator will have to approach through the branches, not by land.

The moose

But their home is not peaceable at the moment. A bull moose is rubbing his antlers on the tree. The squirrels chitter at him, but he pays the tiny animals no attention. He moves away to browse on his own, wading through the water. There is plenty of cover and food in this wetland for the moose. Unlike his cousin the doe, he does not visit the human habitat surrounding and creeping ever closer to his marsh. Most of the townspeople don't even know he is here.

He moved in, quietly, during one summer night three years ago, and has lived contentedly here ever since.

The moose pauses and ducks his head beneath the water's surface, ripping up pond lilies and other freshwater plants. He chews, swallows, and dips down for more.

The muskrat

A muskrat watches the moose from a small hillock that is really his den. Not as skilled an engineer as his cousin the beaver, the muskrat nevertheless does a fine job of creating a lodge out of mud and plants. The muskrat scratches his ear with his hind foot and slips gracefully into the water. He has been asleep in his lodge all day, and now with the setting sun has come out to hunt for frogs and search for water plants.

The opossum

Likewise, the opossum has stirred from his daylong slumber. About a foot long, he is covered with gray fur and has a pointy nose, soft ears, and a hairless tail. He stretches and leaves the nest he slept in last night, beneath the deck of a house that overlooks the wetland. His travels around his territory take him all over this town and south into the next two; he does not go north of the highway. He walks through the yard to the driveway, catching an earthworm on the way. He pauses, ears twitching, alert to every sound. He can hear the roar of traffic some distance away, but nothing nearby. In his short lifetime, the two-year-old opossum has learned that roadways and cars are dangerous. He steps out onto the street, pauses one more time, then hurries across before any cars come.

Forty years ago, no opossums lived in this area. But they're now found throughout the eastern part of the United States and all along the West Coast. Naturally Southern animals, they have a

Opossums, like this youngster, have spread north from their original range and are common sights in the suburbs. Photo by W.L. French, courtesy of the U.S. Fish and Wildlife Service

hard time during cold winters, sometimes losing bits of ears and tails to frostbite.

But on this warm late June evening, the opossum doesn't have to worry about the cold as he roams through backyard after backyard, patrolling his range and looking for food. All is well until he rounds the corner of a garage and comes face to face with another opossum.

It's another male. They hiss at each other, opening their mouths to show off their fifty sharp teeth. They circle each other, still hissing.

Suddenly a bright light interrupts their confrontation—a car is pulling into the driveway. With a last hiss, the two opossums scatter.

"Oh wow!" says the driver to the passenger. "Did you see the size of those rats?"

The bats

Overhead, swifts dip and twirl in the warm air, diving and swooping to catch as many insects as they can before they lose the light completely. They will then retire to their roosts, and the other great insect hunters will take over: the bats.

Two colonies of bats live in the town. The first lives next to the marsh, in an old barn; the other, beneath the highway overpass. The barn colony is made up of little brown bats, and the highway overpass colony consists of big brown bats. Between them, the two colonies consume hundred of pounds of insects every night—making it unnecessary for the Davis family to use insect repellent as they enjoy the evening outside.

Amanda Davis looks up in time to see a little brown bat diving after a moth far overhead. "Look Mom, what's that?"

Her mother looks up, but doesn't recognize the bat for what it is. "That's a nighthawk, honey. It's nothing to be afraid of. Come on, let's go in. It's getting late." As she speaks, she scoops up the remnants of the hot dogs and hamburgers her husband Paul has cooked on the grill and dumps them into a trash can. The three of them head into the house. They lock the doors and shut off the outside light.

The raccoon

As if on cue, the raccoon under the stairs wakes up. He lumbers out from under the porch. He looks fatter than he really is because of his luxurious fur, but he is a bit heavier than his relatives who live in the woods. And that is largely thanks to the Davises. Although they put lids on their trash cans, these aren't much of a challenge for the dexterous raccoon. He pops the lid off effortlessly and reaches in for Amanda's unfinished hot dog, the burnt burger, and the bun that fell on the ground. He licks his lips when he finishes eating and hops down off the can. He sniffs the night air, which tells him of more barbecues, other compost heaps, skunks and muskrats and foxes and coyotes, and all the other residents of this suburb. He sneezes once and walks off to the north. The Davises' day is done, but his has just started.

2. Always a Presence

One type of wildlife has made its home among humans for years: birds.

Many forms of wildlife live among us without our ever seeing them. They conduct their business at night or try hard to avoid human beings altogether. But there's a notable exception, a type of wild creature that lives around us and with us. We like them so much that we don't even mind when their calls wake us up in the morning.

They're birds.

Of all forms of wildlife, birds have the most fans. About 60 million Americans describe themselves as bird watchers. Although some people limit their involvement with birds to tossing bread out onto the garage roof, others take a great interest in the activity around the bird feeders in their backyards. Each bird-feeding household buys about two tons of bird food each year, according to Simon Perkins, an ornithologist with the Massachusetts Audubon Society. Together, bird fans spend about $170 million to feed their favorite creatures.

That's a lot of love.

Why do we love birds so much? Every bird watcher would give you different reasons. In general, we love them for their beauty and the way they bring a bit of wildness into our lives, without the fear that other wildlife species can inspire (such as skunks with the fear of getting sprayed, or raccoons, with the concern about rabies). Feeding the birds lets many people feel they are helping another of the earth's creatures. It also lets us get a close look at these creatures that otherwise wouldn't come near us.

Feeders can be elaborate store-bought creations with contraptions to stymie squirrels, or simple platforms on poles, or even clear plastic containers that attach to the outside of the window with suction cups. Some shapes are easier for small birds, such as chickadees, to feed from, but all feeders have the same goal: getting seed, millet, or other food to the birds.

Who comes to a feeder?

The birds who come to a feeder vary, depending upon what's being served. Sunflower seeds draw evening grosbeaks, doves, goldfinches, titmice, nuthatches, purple finches, house finches, crossbills, and white-throated and white-crowned sparrows. Millet, which is a combination of the seeds of several grass species, will attract blackbirds, doves, juncos, and house sparrows. Thistle seeds will attract chickadees, dark-eyed juncos, song sparrows, house finches, redpolls, pine siskins, purple finches, and white-throated sparrows. Fruit, such as orange slices or raisins, will bring to the feeder orioles, tanagers, thrushes, cedar waxwings, woodpeckers, bluebirds, cardinals, and jays. And corn will attract larger birds, like bobwhites, grackles, and ring-necked pheasants.

Good and bad?

Whenever people watch animals, they quickly develop favorites. For some people, the tiny birds like wrens and titmice are the best part of feeding the birds. Others prefer the bright red cardinal, or the distinguished-looking cedar waxwing.

Believing they're acting in the interest of these favored birds, some people try to encourage only songbirds to use their feeders. They object to the presence of pigeons, house sparrows, starlings, doves, jays, and crows, which they consider "trash birds." They get upset when they spot a bird of prey like a kestrel hovering near the feeder.

There isn't any such thing as a "good bird" or a "bad bird." Just because pigeons, house sparrows and starlings are imported species (that is, humans brought them over from Europe and released them, and they've thrived in the wild), that doesn't make them evil. Crows and jays are considered by some ornithologists to be the smartest members of the bird world. Studies have shown that these birds can actually solve problems and even count, although not very high. And if you ever see a kestrel or other bird of prey catch a bird at your backyard feeder, you may be disturbed by the sight. But remember: the kestrel isn't a bad guy. He's a predator, and he and the other birds all have their roles to play in nature. We'll talk more about the bad reputation that predators have gotten in chapter 6.

You may have heard that feeding birds makes them dependent on human handouts, and if we stop feeding them, the birds will die. That isn't so. Like all living things, birds appreciate a meal they don't need to work for, and they'll come to feeder even at the height of summer, when berries and insects are abundant. But if the feeder was removed, they'd go back to the berries and bugs without a second thought. But that's not to say if you have a feeder you don't have to take care of it. Dirty feeders and spoiled food encourage the growth of bacteria, which in turn can make birds sick or even kill them. So bird-feeder owners should make sure to clean their feeders (and birdbaths) often, and replace old food with fresh, whether the food is a seed mix or fruit.

It's debated whether feeding by people has changed the behavior of some species that used to migrate south come winter, especially the tufted titmouse and the northern cardinal. Warmer winters probably have encouraged these birds to stick around in the north more than bird feeders have. However, our habit of feeding the birds doesn't soften the blow of some of our other activities. We have changed their habitats and, for millions of birds, shortened their lives.

Moving in on birds

As people have expanded their range, they've cut roads through forests, cleared wide swaths of land for power lines, and of course, put in new houses where before there were only trees. This is a process scientists call *habitat fragmentation*, and it's had a tremendous impact on North America's songbirds.

A famous study published in 1959 that was one of the first to recognize this effect looked at Cadiz Township in Wisconsin. Within a period of just seventy years—roughly one person's lifetime—90 percent of the forest was cut down. What remained were tiny pockets of green.

Throughout the eastern United States, 99 percent of what the first European settlers found when they arrived is gone—cut down to clear the way for farms and homes, and used for timber and fuel. The one percent of this old-growth forest that remains is in areas where people couldn't manage to get the logs out—mountain tops and steep ravines. These pristine areas are few and range from 100 acres to 1,000 acres at the most.

What does this mean? Different species of birds occupy different habitats. Some birds do best in the deep forest, while others thrive in the open spaces of meadows and grasslands. Some can live in a small area with a few trees, and others need whole forests to survive.

By clearing the forest so thoroughly, we have removed areas in which birds have nested for years. When we cut down a small forest to build a new housing subdivision, the birds (and other creatures) are driven from the area. What can a bird do?

It may try living in an open area, especially if it's unable to find suitable habitat. But in an unfamiliar place, it may not be able to find enough or the right kind of food, and it can starve. Or it may fall prey to predators.

Or, the bird may find a patch of woods just like the one it had lived in. But if it does, the chances are very high that those woods are already home to birds of the same species. The bird that lost its home may have to fight the resident birds for territory. If it loses, it will be driven away.

Neither of these options sounds promising for the bird, does it?

If the birds are more fortunate, our clearing of the land stops before we reach them. But that opens up a new set of problems.

In many ways, the deep forest is like a castle. Predators such as cats and cowbirds can penetrate the edge, but they rarely forge their way into the deeper parts of the woods—like attacking soldiers who make it across the moat but are stopped short by the castle's walls and towers. The forest-dwelling species are safe in the deep woods, just like the castle's residents are safe inside its innermost keep.

But by clearing the woods, we removed not only the moat but the outside wall of the forest castle—giving the predators a chance to attack the castle's keep.

These creatures include not only our pet cats, but also species that thrive in such "edge" communities, including opossums, skunks, raccoons, jays, crows, and cowbirds. The first five creatures on this list will eat eggs and baby birds in the nest, and some will prey on adult birds when they get the chance.

The cowbird is a predator in a different sense of the word. It is what scientists call a "nest parasite." The female cowbird lays her egg in the nest of a different species, pushing out the eggs of the resident female. When the cowbird egg hatches, the other bird raises the chick as if it were her own. By using other birds to raise her young, the female cowbird can have many offspring without having to invest the time and energy to raise them.

Another problem with habitat fragmentation, besides exposing birds to predators they never had to deal with before, is that some species need not just unbroken forest or grassland habitat, but lots of it. Leaving a few trees undisturbed or a couple of lots of land without houses built on them isn't enough when you're talking about species like the grasshopper sparrow or the upland sandpiper. Both birds need lots of open grassland habitat to survive: for the grasshopper sparrow, 30 acres is the minimum. For the upland sandpiper, 200 acres is the least amount of land the bird can thrive on.

Just as much as they need their habitats protected, birds need their lives defended, right in our own backyards, against a voracious and destructive predator that we unleash on them daily: our pet cats.

The threat of Tabby

See that cat sitting on the deck, his eyes half closed as he dozes in the sun? It's hard to believe that he and his kind could be to blame

A house cat stalks through tall grass. A successful hunter can bring down a few songbirds a day. Courtesy of the publisher

for the deaths of millions of songbirds a year, isn't it? But if your cat goes outdoors, chances are he does kill birds while he's prowling, even if he never brings them home to you.

Both history and recent studies have shown that cats can have a huge impact on bird populations.

All members of the feline family are fine hunters, and the domestic cat is no exception. The cat's hearing is better than that of humans or dogs, tuned to pick up the faintest squeak or rustle. A room that's pitch dark to us looks to a cat as if it's lit by the full moon. Combined with the silent step of its softly padded paws, the cat's senses make it one of the animal world's most skilled and efficient predators. For thousands of years, humans have taken advantage of this skill to control populations of mice in cities and towns, farms and fields. But in the suburban wilds, the cat may be *too* good at what it does.

Concern about the cat's effect on wildlife isn't new. More than 100 years ago, the famous naturalist Charles Darwin connected the abundance of clover to the presence of elderly women in an English village. The more elderly women, the more pet cats; the more cats, the fewer mice. Fewer mice in turn led to more bumblebees (which the mice ate), and that meant more clover, which depended on the bees for pollination. It may seem unlikely that a pet cat can affect the world around it, but Darwin's observations show that it's true: Our activities, including those of the animals we keep, can and do change things, and not always for the better.

In 1894, a lighthouse keeper's cat was responsible for the discovery of a new bird species in New Zealand, the Stephen's Island wren. Unfortunately, the discovery was made because the cat caught and killed the wren—so the extinction of a species immediately followed its discovery.

In 1916, American naturalist Edward Howe Forbush said that a mature cat could catch about fifty birds a year "in good hunting grounds." Based on figures he got from wildlife officials, Forbush estimated that cats killed eight million birds a year in just Massachusetts, New York, and Illinois.

In the early 1990s, two biologists studied the cats of Felmersham, an English village. Of the village's seventy-eight cat owners, seventy-seven agreed to save their cats' prey for the scientists. By the end of the year, they had collected 1,090 prey "items." Of that total, 17 percent were wood mice, 16 percent were house sparrows and 14 percent were field voles. The rest included rabbits, shrews, blackbirds, robins, and thrushes. Working from these figures, the scientists estimated that English cats kill 70 million animals each year.

An American study of birds done by the Cornell University Laboratory of Ornithology found that pet cats were second only to sharp-shinned hawks in the number of birds taken at feeders. Cats were involved in about a third of the 567 incidents observed.

Wildlife ecologist Stanley Temple has called domestic cats "the principal mammalian predator of birds in North America." An expert on rare and declining species, he spent four years studying cats and their effect on birds in rural Wisconsin. Based on what he learned, he figures that cats in Wisconsin kill 7.8 million birds a year.

You can do your part to help cut down on this threat to birds, especially if you have a feeder. First off, if you own a cat, try to keep it indoors. Besides protecting the birds, you'll be protecting your pet, too: indoor cats live longer than cats that go out, where they can pick up parasites and diseases, or, worse, be hit by a car.

You won't be being cruel to your cat, especially if it's a kitten who has never gone prowling outdoors before. He won't know what he's missing. An older cat will probably object to having to stay in (and will try to escape, too, no doubt), but be patient and your cat will adjust.

Another step you can take to help out the birds is to look at the location of the feeder or birdbath. Is it located near shrubbery or tall grass that might conceal a cat, whether pet or stray? If so, try moving the feeder or birdbath so the birds that are using it can spot Tabby coming.

You can also try putting a collar on your cat. Birds are very visual creatures, and if the collar is brightly colored or has a wild design, the birds may actually be able to spot the collar before they spot the cat. A bell on the collar can help alert birds and other small animals, like mice, to the cat's presence, too.

A towering problem

Another threat birds are facing in today's world is the proliferation of radio, TV, and cellular-phone transmission towers. These towers stand hundreds of feet tall and are supported by cables that stretch from the tower to the ground. Ornithologist Simon Perkins explains that migrating birds fly into these towers and kill themselves. "During certain conditions, you can drive up in the morning to the base of a tower and find dozens or hundreds of birds that have killed themselves," he says. In bad weather, birds that normally fly thousands of feet above the ground fly lower and hit the tower or supporting cables because they never see the structures. Perkins says this problem has been recognized just within the last few years, and so far no solutions have been found.

Not always a match made in heaven

Although widely loved, birds can sometimes come into conflict with people. They can build their nests in gutters, which can lead to water damage if the nest plugs up the water flow. They can eat berries and other fruit right off the trees. And it's a rare driver who hasn't been left a "present" on his windshield when he's parked his car beneath a tree.

Bird problems, like wildlife problems in general, can be solved with patience and creativity.

Remember: It is against federal law to harm any songbird. All wild birds except house sparrows, starlings, and pigeons are protected by U.S. law. You can't trap them, catch them, or kill them.

Keeping birds out of areas where they aren't wanted is the best technique. For example, if a pair of sparrows nested in a gutter at your house last year, your family can install "gutter guards" before they return to build again. These guards keep out leaves and pine needles (and birds!) but allow rain water to flow into the gutters. Birds that are nesting in clothes dryer vents can also be excluded by using hardware cloth (a kind of wire mesh) over the vent opening.

It's vital to be patient when using these methods, especially if the birds are raising young. Let the babies leave the nest before you close it off.

Scare techniques can also work well. Scare tape, a shiny metallic ribbon, flashes as the wind moves it and can keep birds away from fruit trees or, when laid across a surface, keep them from perching where they aren't wanted. Mylar balloons can work, too.

One thing that doesn't work very well in keeping birds away are plastic hawks and owls. I once passed by a house with a plastic owl on its roof. Keeping the owl company was a flock of two dozen pigeons.

Although birds may occasionally do something we don't like, most of the time we're happy to see them. Each of them consumes thousands of insects a year. They add beauty to our world. However, one large bird is the target of a lot of dislike in the United States right now, even though just a few years ago spotting one filled people with delight. This is the Canada goose. It and the beaver are thriving among us—to some people's dismay.

3. Joy or Nuisance?

When does love turn into hate? And how can you change it back again?

They are a sure sign of the changing seasons: Vs of honking geese flying high overhead, either returning north to their breeding grounds in arctic Canada or heading south to wait out the winter in warmer climes. Not so long ago, an arrow of geese would make everyone who saw it stop what they were doing and gaze up in wonder.

Canada geese aren't such a rare sight anymore. In fact, if you go to a local pond, lake, reservoir, golf course, or even soccer field, your chances of seeing these very adaptable birds are excellent. Sometimes, too good.

The Canada goose has quickly gone from virtue to varmint in the eyes of some people. But that's not just the goose's fault. Human beings played a role in the goose's comeback, too.

Today, roughly a million Canada geese inhabit the eastern part of the United States, the area that ornithologists call the Atlantic Flyway. The geese fall into two types. About 10 percent of them are migrating geese—the ones who form those lovely Vs in the autumn sky. The rest are resident geese. They're a different subspecies of Canada goose from the migrant birds (in fact, one scientist believes they should be classified as an entirely different species). Scientists classify the migrant birds as *Branta canadensis*; the resident birds are mostly *Branta canadensis maxima*, or the giant Canada goose. And giant they are, weighing at their biggest 24 pounds (the average is about 12 pounds) and standing about four feet tall, with wingspans of about six feet. These big birds originally were found in the midwestern areas of the United States and Canada. They migrated little, because their larger size made it easier for them to endure winter weather that drives smaller Canadas north in the summer and south in the winter.

Back from the edge of extinction

Human settlers found the giant Canada geese to be irresistible targets, and hunted the birds intensely. By the turn of the twentieth century, scientists believed that the subspecies had been made extinct by hunting.

Then in the 1960s, a small flock of giant Canadas was found in captivity—living on the grounds of the Mayo Clinic in Rochester, Minnesota, where patients enjoyed watching them. Scientists, excited about the subspecies' rediscovery and trying to keep these birds from becoming extinct, transported them around the country to establish colonies, according to Rich Malecki and Paul Curtis of the Cornell University Laboratory of Ornithology. But the world of the 1960s was very different from the world that had driven the birds to the edge of extinction—and this new world was actually favorable to the big birds.

Migrant birds have it tough. Not only is migration itself physically exhausting, but also during the trip they face the dangers of hunters (in fact, Malecki notes, recently there have been closed hunting seasons on Canada geese because hunters were taking too many birds). The arctic environment where they hatch their goslings is demanding—there they must deal with finding sufficient food for themselves and their offspring and protect themselves from predators. Then they must fly south again. These physical stresses make the birds mature more slowly than their resident cousins (migrant birds don't have goslings until they're four or five years old). Not all of them live long enough to have offspring, and those that do don't enjoy as long a life as a resident Canada does.

So when that remnant colony of resident geese was spread around by the scientists, suddenly, the birds found themselves in a highly favorable environment. For a change, their habit of remaining in the same area year round didn't work against them by making them a target—because now they were staying in areas where people lived and where hunting was forbidden. The food in these areas is plentiful and good—it's usually grass grazed from lawns nicely maintained by people. In addition, few predators threaten them in their suburban homes. In short, everything that makes life tough for a migratory Canada goose—environment, food, predators, and breeding challenges—works in favor of these resident birds.

They live to about the age of twenty, although some older birds have been found. Because they live longer, resident Canada geese raise lots of goslings. These goslings mature more quickly than their migrant cousins, and are ready to have youngsters of their own within a couple of years of hatching.

Houses ring this pond in Lynnfield, Massachusetts, where giant Canada geese have successfully produced a large number of goslings.
Photo by the author

How many geese?

Canadas didn't annoy people right away. In fact, they were really quite welcomed. Golfers enjoyed seeing the magnificent brown, black and white birds along the fairways of their favorite courses. Joggers liked to watch the big birds cruise the waters of the ponds they ran beside. Families loved to take loaves of bread to the ponds and lakes where the geese lived and feed them.

Because they were welcomed, the geese settled in to raise families. And that's where the trouble started. In the 1980s, for reasons nobody knows, the resident Canada goose population took off.

A few Canada geese can create a lot of Canada geese in a relatively short span of time; Rich Malecki notes that they can double their numbers in just five years.

Let's say three mated pairs of Canada geese take up residence on your school soccer field. Each year, each pair raises five goslings (clutches range in size from just one egg to as many as fifteen; five is about average), so at the end of the first year, the three pairs have raised fifteen young.

At the end of two years, each pair will have produced ten young geese, or thirty total. That's not too bad, right? Well, in year number three, things have begun to get interesting, because the first generation of goslings have grown up, and now have their own goslings.

In about five years, three pairs of geese and their offspring could produce about 285 new geese. The soccer field would be pretty crowded by that point. (Of course, this model doesn't take into account birds that die from injuries, such as being hit by cars, or birds that don't successfully reproduce.) But you get the idea: Over ten or fifteen years, you can get hundreds of geese from a single pair.

The root of the problem

All these geese might eat a lot of grass off the soccer field. But what most people object to is what happens after the geese eat the grass: it's passed out of their bodies as feces. Goose feces are blackish-green, about two inches long, and slippery. Each goose passes about a pound of feces a day. (They've been described as eating and pooping machines.) A family flock can consist of twenty or thirty birds, and during the molting season (when the adult birds lose their flight feathers), a number of family groups will congregate in the same place—resulting in a flock of 500 birds or more! That means a lot of grass gets eaten and a lot of feces get passed.

Goose feces can mess up sidewalks, golf courses, lawns, and playgrounds. Not only do the feces make taking a walk near a goose pond a challenge, they can also raise the bacteria counts in that pond. This bacteria is called fecal coliform bacteria, or *Escherichia coli*, (called *E. coli* for short). If a person swims in or drinks water contaminated by these bacteria, he can get quite sick. The more geese, the more feces, and the more contaminated the water can become.

Managing Canada geese is difficult, explains Malecki, because it's impossible to tell the subspecies—or the sexes—apart. A male giant Canada goose may be pretty easy to spot, especially when he weighs 20 pounds or more. But a female giant Canada goose is about the same size as a male migratory goose, and males and females have the same plumage, or feather coloring. So when you're looking at Canada geese, it's hard to tell exactly what kind of Canada goose you're looking at!

Despite this challenge, wildlife experts have devised several ideas for dealing with these big birds. Some work better than others, but some upset people.

One of the simplest and most effective ways of cutting down on the number of geese in an area is to discourage people from feeding them. Any animal appreciates a free meal. If the free meals are a regular thing, animals are smart enough to figure that out and know that it's going to be worth their while to hang around. But if that source of easy food is removed, the animals will soon realize it and go elsewhere.

(It's amazing how many human-wildlife conflicts begin with humans feeding the wildlife. You'll read more about this misguided good intention in the chapters about deer and predators, in the case of the coyote.)

However, we provide even more food for geese than the odd loaf of bread. How? Just take a look at the expansive swaths of green that make up our suburban lawns and golf courses. We may just see grass, but the geese see a supermarket!

Americans love their lawns, and they spend a great deal of time and money taking care of them and getting them to look just so. For some folks, lawn care—fertilizing, watering, mowing—is their major weekend activity. Lawn care is big business: not only do commercial lawn companies do very well in the United States (in 1987 they earned $2.8 billion), but do-it-yourselfers spend lots of cash on lawn-care products. Scotts, a major producer of grass seed, fertilizers, and chemical pest control products for lawns, reported sales of $1.113 billion in 1998.

With all this money and time invested, people really don't like having the geese grazing their lawn.

An easy way to solve this is to not have a lawn. Geese like lawns not only for their delicious and well-fed grass, but also because the short-mown blades of grass send up lots of tender new shoots. The short grass also makes spotting any potential predators easier, too. If people let their lawns grow tall (geese dislike walking through plants that are 18 inches tall or more), or turn them into meadows, the geese won't come to dine. The homeowner may have to deal with remarks from the neighbors. (But the homeowner can get help from the National Wildlife Federation in educating his or her neighbors; more about that in chapter 7.) But by following this "natural" landscaping, the homeowner may discover that not only are there no geese to be concerned with, but also he or she will save money on the water bill because native species of grasses and plants don't need as much water (or fertilizer) as the traditional lawn does.

Letting the grass grow isn't really feasible for the people who run golf courses or maintain public parks. But there is a chemical repellent that seems to work quite well—it's called methyl anthranilate, or MA, and it's made from Concord grapes. Sprayed on the grass, it makes the grass taste bitter and the geese dislike it. MA wears off quickly, though, and has to be reapplied every couple of weeks or after the grass is mowed. It's also expensive, costing about $95 a gallon to treat an acre.

Visual repellents can work well, too. Flags, scare tape, Mylar balloons, and rapidly flashing strobe lights have all been found to deter geese from settling into an area. However, geese will get used to these objects, especially when they realize they aren't going to be hurt. Moving the repellents around or using different ones at different times is necessary to keep the birds wary and away.

In less populated areas, geese can be kept away through the use of noisemakers, like cannons, sirens, and fireworks. However, these methods aren't usually appreciated by suburban residents!

Fencing off areas can make them less accessible to geese, especially if the fence lies between the body of water the geese use and the grass they like to graze. Barriers don't have to be elaborate—they can be as simple as hay bales arranged to block the path from the water to the grass. Researchers discovered that geese also dislike tall vegetation or boulders placed along the shore, because it blocks their view.

An innovative method for keeping geese away from where they aren't wanted uses one of human's oldest allies: the dog, specifically, the trained border collie. Border collies are experts at sheep herding, and it turns out that they are quite good at goose herding, too. The dogs are used just to frighten the geese, not catch them, and aren't used during the molting season (because then the geese can't fly and get away). The geese soon get the message that a place with a dog is not a place they want to stay, so they'll move elsewhere.

Keeping down the population

Repellents, dogs, and fences can do a good job of keeping geese away, but they don't cut down on the number born each year.

Wildlife managers keep looking for ways to control the goose population. There are three basic tacks they can take:

- Reducing the number of eggs that are laid;
- Reducing the number of eggs that hatch; or
- Reducing the number of adult birds.

Traditionally, part of the population of adult birds would fall each year to hunters' guns. For the migratory Canadas, this is still the case. But the resident birds have the advantage of living in populated areas, where the use of firearms is prohibited by law. Adult birds are sometimes hit by cars, or may be caught by a dog if they aren't paying attention, but overall, resident adult geese have few predators to fear. As a result, the geese live long lives.

Some states have started using "goose roundups" as a way to control goose numbers. Roundups are held during the molting period, from about mid-June to mid-July. In a roundup, entire flocks of birds are shooed into pens or nets on shore.

The captured geese may be translocated—that is, taken to another site and released there. The problem with translocation is that few places are willing to take the geese, as they have plenty of their own.

Another tactic is to separate the males and females and create single-sex flocks. In theory, this sounds like a good idea (after all, an all-male or all-female flock can't reproduce). However, the geese may find their way home again to join the opposite-sex members, or attract new mates. This method is time consuming, because it's impossible to tell males from females without a close examination, and it doesn't work for very long.

In Michigan for the last twenty years, the giant Canada geese caught in roundups have been taken to slaughterhouses and killed. Their meat is given to homeless shelters and poor families. The problem is, the roundups haven't done much of anything to reduce the number of geese, says John Hadidian of the Humane Society of the United States (HSUS). It may remove a flock from an area, but it's very likely that the area will soon be discovered by another flock—sometimes in as little as two weeks! Killing adult birds—even if their meat is used to feed hungry people—is not a popular solution with the public, and the HSUS does not support it.

Another method is controlling the number of eggs that hatch. This method is done in a few different ways. All of them use the bird's instinct to incubate an egg until it hatches.

One method is to remove the eggs from the nest and replace them with wooden dummy eggs. The female goose will sit on, or brood, the eggs. If the eggs were removed from the nest and no dummy eggs put in, she would just lay another clutch of eggs and raise them instead. Because she thinks she is sitting on a full clutch of real eggs, she won't lay any more. But of course, the dummy eggs never hatch. Eventually, the female gives up and abandons the nest; she and her mate will have produced no offspring this year.

If they successfully raise a family one year, birds will return to a nesting site the next year. By not hatching these eggs, these Canada geese may look for a new nest site next season—possibly in a different pond.

Instead of using dummy eggs, wildlife managers may tamper with the real goose eggs so they won't hatch. Shaking an egg hard will destroy the embryo inside; this is called "addling." Poking a long, sharp pin through the eggshell introduces bacteria into the egg, and the bacteria kill the embryo. Or, the egg gets coated with corn oil; the oil clogs up the pores in the shell that allow air and moisture to pass in and out of the egg, and the embryo dies.

Although these methods may sound cruel, they're less objectionable to the HSUS than the roundups are, and they keep the goose population down.

Despite their tarnished reputation with people, there are still few animals as magical as the Canada goose. They're one of our most distinguished-looking waterfowl. Their flying Vs remind us of the seasons' changes. And even if they don't migrate, their rusty, honking call conjures up dreams of a wilder time, and can still set the human heart to dancing.

Beavers building

What does North America's largest rodent, the beaver, have in common with the Canada goose?

Like the Canada goose, the beaver was also near extinction, hunted to the brink for its fur. And like the Canada goose, the beaver has made a comeback.

The beaver (*Castor canadensis*) is a member of the same group as squirrels, mice, guinea pigs, and porcupines. Its brown fur is thick and waterproof, and its broad, flat tail and feet are black. Beavers spend much of their time in the water, and their webbed feet make them excellent swimmers,

They live in family groups inside a lodge built of branches and sticks. The entrances to the lodge are underwater, which makes it hard for enemies to get in.

Probably no other animal (except humans) has such an effect on its environment as the beaver does. The dams they build across streams and rivers create wetlands that support a huge variety of life, according to Susan Langlois of the Massachusetts Department of Fisheries and Wildlife. "Beaver flowages are incredibly productive environments," she says. Insects, songbirds, small mammals, muskrats, mink, deer, and even bear find food and shelter in the marshy areas that the beaver dam creates.

Besides creating great habitats for other creatures, the beavers' wetlands have the additional advantage of being nature's filters, cleansing water as it flows through the stalks and roots of myriad plants.

And in today's world, where we are losing wetlands every day, the beaver is a blessing, notes John Hadidian of the Humane Society of the United States. "Beaver do so many good things for us, we should be trying to keep them here," Hadidian says. Imagine, he says: the beaver does for free what the government is spending millions of dollars to accomplish—restoring wetlands. In addition, human-restored wetlands don't function as well as those created by beavers, notes Stephanie Hagopian, coordinator of the Living with Wildlife Program run by the Massachusetts Society for the Prevention of Cruelty to Animals (MSPCA), although no one is sure why.

Not everyone is happy to see beaver arrive, however. For some, the reason is as simple as not liking how the beaver dam looks on their property. In others, the water backed up by the beaver dam floods a house's septic tank—and then the family's drinking water well. The dam prevents the water from flowing, and still water can be a huge nursery for mosquitoes. Or, the water may flood a street or road, making it impossible to drive on or even washing it out completely.

It's a collision of nature's great builders: beavers and people.

A beaver's life

Beavers are family-oriented animals. A mated pair has one litter of babies, or "kits," a year. Sometimes they have as few as one kit, other times, as many as five. If good-quality food is in short supply, the beavers will have fewer young, or no young at all.

When young beavers are about three years of age, they leave their parents' pond and set off to find their own place. The needs of a beaver are very particular. There must be trees, for not only do the beavers need the wood to build with, but also they need the bark and leaves for food. They eat birch, aspen, alder and willow, as well as water lilies and other aquatic plants. As far as the landscape is concerned, beavers like areas that are flat and fertile, with a stream running through them.

When a beaver (or a pair of beavers) finds an ideal spot, it will start to construct its colony, consisting of a dam and its lodge. More than likely, it won't be the first beaver to have ever set up housekeeping in this spot. Beavers maintain their colonies until they have cut down all the trees they can safely reach (they don't like getting too far from the safety of the water). Then they'll abandon the colony and seek a new home elsewhere. And with their leaving a new cycle begins in the life of the colony. Once a wetland, it will begin to fill in, and gradually becomes a meadow. Over time, trees encroach on the meadow. Once again, the forest has returned—and it may look much like it did when the beaver first found it decades before. Not surprisingly, the forest will attract another beaver, who will continue the work that his predecessor left off.

Large pipes bridge a beaver dam in Peabody, Massachusetts, in an effort to control the amount of flooding the dam causes. Photo by the author

They're a natural

Building is in the beavers' blood. Nobody can stop a beaver from building—it's like asking a bird not to fly. Tear a hole in a dam and the beaver will have it patched within a few hours. Some people have even blown up dams with dynamite (which is illegal), but the beavers built right back. Even if road workers clear beavers' handiwork from drainage culverts, the beavers will soon have the blockage back in place. Although nobody's quite certain what makes a beaver build, Paul Curtis of Cornell University and his fellow researchers suspect that the feel of the moving water—that is, the speed the water's flowing—triggers the beavers to build in certain places but not in others.

Beavers use their strong yellow incisor teeth to cut down trees. The beaver digs its top incisors into the tree, and then drives its lower teeth in, too. When it has a good grip, the beaver rips out the piece of wood and spits it out to the side. This logging method is so effective that a beaver can fell a tree with a six-inch diameter trunk within minutes.

Using the logs, branches, and lots of mud from the pond bottom, the beaver builds its dam. The dam starts below the water and stretches across the stream. A finished beaver dam is strong enough for a person to walk on, and holds back thousands of pounds of water. The beavers' lodge is constructed in much the same way.

Beavers don't have much to worry about in the way of natural predators. The wolves and cougars that may have caught them in the past have been long gone from the beaver's range. Their main predator today is people, who trap them for their luxurious fur. In the past, beaver pelts were extremely valuable, and there is still a market for them today. However, trapping is less and less acceptable in the eyes of the public. Proof of that is the 1996 Massachusetts law that made it illegal to catch beavers in leg-hold traps. (Beavers can still be caught, but in suitcase-size traps that are more expensive than the old leg-hold traps.) California outlawed trapping in 1998. With the passage of such laws, some wildlife managers are scratching their heads about what to do with the beaver now.

We need to find a way that will let the beaver build but keep the water from becoming a problem.

In Peabody, Massachusetts, there's a pond called Devil's Dishful. And in this pond live beavers. Around this pond live people. A recipe for disaster? No. The people and the beavers of Devil's Dishful have found a way to live in peace with each other, thanks to the efforts of local residents, including Mary de La Valette and John M. Leslie. The work of these "Friends of Devil's Dishful" shows what average people can do. John is a retired breeder and trainer of German Shepherd dogs. Mary works at a group home for retarded adults.

In the mid-1990s, the town's conservation commission, acting on complaints from some residents, voted to trap the pond's beavers. Mary, John, and other concerned people rallied to the beavers' defense, and the commissioners agreed to look at different options.

The solution has been to install "beaver deceivers." These devices are combinations of pipes, which encourage water flow through dams, and large, trapezoid-shaped cages that prevent the beavers from successfully blocking the pipes. They were developed and installed by Skip Lyle, a wildlife biologist from the state of Maine (which, according to the MSPCA's Stephanie Hagopian, enjoys a 95 percent success rate in using beaver deceivers and other non-lethal methods in conflicts).

One deceiver is in place in the pond, and several others are located upstream from the pond, to encourage the flow of water. Not only are the human and beaver residents of the area pleased with the outcome, but dozens of bird species (including egrets, great blue herons, and kingfishers) and other kinds of animals, such as muskrats, now call the pond system home.

John visits the pond daily to check on the water level and clear away eelgrass and other vegetation the beavers may have lodged up

This "beaver deceiver"—sometimes called a "beaver baffler"—prevents nature's builders from damming up the culvert that runs beneath a nearby road. Its wire grate construction and angled sides are difficult for beavers to block. In addition, each day local residents clear away any building materials the beavers lodge against the deceiver. Photo by the author

against the deceiver. "I really enjoy it," he says. "I think the city has a jewel here."

Without the work of people like him, there wouldn't be any beavers at the pond, and very likely there wouldn't be the variety of wildlife there is today.

A battle of wits

It takes lots of human ingenuity to find a workable solution that won't end up with the beavers or their dams being destroyed.

Skip Hilliker, the beaver consultant to the Fund for Animals, used to trap beavers. He stopped in 1985, when he took in a beaver kit orphaned when its mother was killed in a trap. "They are the most amazing animal we have in this country today," Hilliker says.

As part of his work, Hilliker works with Laura Simon, urban wildlife expert for the Fund for Animals, in dealing with beaver complaints. Because beavers are so clever at construction, they easily dam up many human inventions meant to allow water to flow through their dams and eliminate flooding problems. After years of experimenting, Hilliker hit on using two lengths of PVC pipe (the white plastic pipe that plumbers use) and covering the ends with wire mesh (so the beavers can't plug the pipes). He sets the pipes in notches he cuts into the dam. Unlike some other solutions, Hilliker's method is inexpensive (materials cost about $15 and can be bought just about anywhere), and quick (he's installed the pipes in some spots in about twenty minutes).

Sometimes it's just a matter of getting people to appreciate nature. "People's inclination up front is to kill the animal," says Stephanie Hagopian. She often visits people who are having conflicts with beavers to tell them about the good that beavers do, and to encourage them to look at the animals as a joy, rather than a nuisance. She tries to teach people about their animal neighbors. "I've had people call me saying 'There's this furry thing in my back yard,'" she says, "And when we've talked for a while, they realize it's not going to hurt them, and maybe even do something good for them, they say, 'Hey, wow, that's really neat.'"

And what could have been a nuisance becomes a joy.

4. Deer, Deer, Everywhere

Back from near-extinction, deer are the largest mammals we share our habitat with. But we don't always share willingly.

Most of the creatures that share our neighborhoods are relatively small. Squirrels weigh about a pound. Woodchucks tip the scales at about four pounds. And even a red fox, with its long bushy tail, weighs only about as much as a house cat.

But one animal neighbor, the whitetail deer, can stand six feet tall and weigh as much as 200 pounds. Its bigger cousin, the moose, stands an astounding nine feet tall and can weigh 1,800 pounds. The sheer size of these animal neighbors makes dealing with them a whole different ball game.

North America is home to three members of the deer family: the mule deer, the whitetail deer, and the moose. The whitetail

A deer hesitates before crossing a road. About 500,000 deer are hit by cars in the U.S. each year. Photo by Gary M. Stolz, courtesy of the U.S. Fish and Wildlife Service

deer, *Odocoileus virginanus*, is the most common deer in the East, while the mule deer (*Odocoileus hemionus*) is more often found in the western United States. They look much alike, but the mule deer has larger ears and a black or black-tipped tail, while the whitetail has—you guessed it—a white tail (and just to keep things interesting, Nature has made the western version of the whitetail deer with a black tail, so it's called the blacktail deer). Neither the whitetail or the mule deer will ever be confused with the moose (*Alces alces*). The moose is the largest member of the deer family, larger than even the elk or the caribou. It has broad antlers, a large nose, and a "beard" hanging from its chin.

Mule deer tend to stay clear of human settlements, preferring the solitude of the western wilderness to close contact with people, their pets, and their yards and gardens. Moose enter human-dominated areas once in a while, usually in spring, when young moose are moving to find new territories. Neither the mule deer nor the moose comes into contact—and conflict—with people as often as the whitetail does.

As opposed to occasional visits from moose, whitetails truly do live among people. Scientists have discovered that some deer live their whole lives in a five-block area of suburbia. Entranced by their beauty, humans have encouraged their presence with handouts of food. Realizing that the food was good and the area safe (suburbs contain few predators, whether animal or human), whitetails have settled in to stay. They have thrived among us, and their numbers have increased.

An amazing comeback

Believe it or not, at the beginning of the twentieth century whitetail deer were on their way to being extinct in the United States. About half a million survived in the country, and some states, such as Connecticut and Rhode Island, had no deer at all.

It was a tremendous decline from the deer's population before the arrival of European settlers, which is estimated to have been between 23 million and 34 million. Besides being preyed on by wolves, cougars, and bears, millions of deer fell to human hunters as well. According to one estimate, the eastern Indian tribes killed 4.5 to over 6 million deer every year.

However, the arrival of the Europeans turned up the heat. Guns—even those as inefficient and difficult to aim as colonial weapons—allowed the colonists to kill deer more quickly than ever before. Farmers cleared land for crops. The effect on the deer population of these new pressures was quickly apparent. As early as 1694, Massachusetts introduced a "closed season" in which deer could not be hunted. By the time of the Revolutionary

War, all the American colonies (except Georgia) had such a closed season.

Some hunting was for food and skins, but some of it was just for sport, and the dead deer were left in the woods and fields. This kind of wasteful hunting reached its peak in the 1800s, when humankind waged war on all America's animal species. The whitetail deer was among the victims. Even though deer are quick to reproduce, not even they could withstand this on-slaught. Their numbers dwindled. By the start of the twentieth century, about 500,000 whitetail deer remained. Sighting a deer was a rare occurrence.

What saved the whitetail? Curiously enough, part of what saved them were their human hunters. No, they didn't all agree to stop hunting—although the law-abiding ones observed the rules insti-tuted about how many deer they could kill and when they could hunt them. Instead, they helped bring the deer and many other an-imals back through the Pittman-Robertson Act, also known as the Federal Aid in Wildlife Restoration Act.

Congress passed the Pittman-Robertson Act in 1937, when the outlook for many kinds of wildlife was bleak. It imposed excise taxes on guns and ammunition (and later, on bow-hunting equip-ment). This tax money went to support wildlife research and habi-tat restoration. The act also insured that the fees the states collected for hunting licenses went to the state's wildlife programs and were not spent on other things.

Today, the whitetail deer population has bounced back from its record low to a total of about 20 million deer in the United States. More deer, of course, means more chance of encountering a deer—it's just common sense.

A deer's favorite foods

According to Cornell University, these common garden plants are likely to get eaten by deer.

Trees	Shrubs, bushes and flowers
Apple	American arborvitae
Atlantic white cedar	Clematis
Balsam fir	English ivy
Cherry	Evergreen azaleas
Eastern hemlock	Hostas
Eastern white pine	Hydrangea
European mountain ash	Lilacs
Fraser fir	Old-fashioned weigela
Norway maple	Privet
Plum	Rhododendrons
Saucer magnolia	Rose of Sharon
Sweet mock orange	Roses
Willows	Viburnum
	Wintercreeper
	Yew

Setting the table for a deer's banquet

Deer are browsers. That means they tend to eat leaves and flowers off shrubs and other woody plants. (Grazers, in contrast, eat grass; horses and cows are both grazers.) They especially like ornamental plants that people use to landscape their backyards and vegetable gardens.

Some people spend thousands of dollars on landscaping their properties—certain kinds of trees can cost more than $5,000 each.

Others own orchards and make their living from selling the fruit. When deer eat these plants or when bucks damage them by rubbing them with their antlers, the people can lose a great deal of money.

When a landscaping plant gets eaten, people's impulse is to go to the nursery and buy another one to replace it. But as one deer expert said, this is like doing the deer's food shopping—the second plant gets eaten just as the first one did! Probably the best way to keep deer from browsing on plants is to decorate the yard with plants they don't especially like. These include barberry, paper birch, common boxwood, American holly, Colorado blue spruce, and Russian olive. Other possibilities include honey locust, Chinese holly, inkberry, mountain laurel, common sassafras, and flowering dogwood. Animal welfare organizations, including the Humane Society of the United States and the Massachusetts Society for the Prevention of Cruelty to Animals, encourage people to try putting in plants like these.

A stinky situation

However, using different plants isn't always an option—for example, if a person owns an apple orchard. In that case, *repellents* might work. Repellents are compounds that keep deer away from plants. They include chemical repellents and visual repellents.

Chemical repellents are compounds that try to drive the deer away by making the plants taste or smell bad. They can be homemade or store-bought. If the latter, they have to be approved for use by the Environmental Protection Agency, and people using them have to be careful to follow directions: Certain repellents are approved for use on some plants but not on others, especially fruit trees and vegetables that people will be eating.

Some chemical repellents, like Ro-Pel (denatonium saccharide), make the plant bitter. Capsaicin (the chemical that makes jalapeños and other peppers *hot!*) is another taste repellent; it makes the plant too spicy to eat. Rotten egg solids are a taste and *odor* repellent—you can imagine why that works—and garlic has been used effectively to keep deer from eating plants.

Among the homemade deer repellents that people use are bags of human or dog hair and bars of soap. Hung from the branches of the trees or bushes the deer are browsing on, the smell of these objects can keep deer away.

Visual repellents work by scaring the deer. Deer are naturally cautious and avoid unfamiliar or startling things. Scare tape is a shiny metallic ribbon that twists in the breeze, and the resulting lightshow unnerves deer. Shiny metallic balloons have the same effect.

Other people get dogs to keep deer at bay.

The problem with repellents, whether chemical, visual, or canine, is that deer can get used to them. Once they learn that the scare tape isn't going to attack them, they're no longer afraid of it. John D. McDonald, a deer expert with the Massachusetts Department of Fisheries and Wildlife, says that he has seen a deer browsing just five feet away from a barking dog. (The dog, which was on a chain, was much more excited than deer was, McDonald recalls). So for repellents to work, people must use different kinds, and move them around frequently.

Taking the o-fence-ive

How about a fence? Won't that keep the deer away from the plants altogether? Yes, and no.

Fences are the most effective way to keep deer out of an area. But not just any fence will do, because deer are excellent jumpers and can easily clear a six-foot-tall fence—and have been known to jump fences ten feet high! They'll also crawl underneath a fence that's nine inches off the ground, such as a single-strand electric

A fence is no problem for this whitetail deer. Deer have been known to clear fences as high as ten feet. Courtesy of the U.S. Fish and Wildlife Service

fence. Fences may have to be very tall or very broad to keep deer out, and can be expensive to install.

However, they don't hurt the deer and save the house owner the problem of dealing with smelly or unattractive repellents in the yard.

Road hazards

Along Route 93 in New Hampshire, diamond-shaped yellow signs dot the roadsides. "Moose Crossing," they say. In other spots, large rectangular signs urge drivers, "Brake for Moose: It Could Save Your Life." Throughout the country, diamond-shaped signs bearing the silhouette of a leaping buck are becoming more common sights.

Hitting a moose or a deer with an automobile results in a terrible accident that can not only kill the animal, but far too often, the people in the car as well. According to insurance industry estimates, about half a million deer are struck by cars on America's roadways every year (remember, at the beginning of the twentieth century that would have been the *total* population of whitetails). Besides the deaths and injuries to deer and to people, these collisions cause $1 billion a year in damage to cars and trucks. That's a lot of money.

Accidents often happen when deer are most active—at dusk, at night and in the early morning. The animal begins to cross the road and gets surprised by an oncoming car, or may even dart from the shoulder into the car's path. Sometimes the driver tries to swerve and avoid the deer, and the deer, not knowing which way to go, turns and runs back the way it came. The swerving car plows right into it.

Nighttime drivers must be especially alert for moose, because their large bodies are high up on their long legs, out of the range of a car's headlights. Many drivers who hit moose never see them until seconds before impact.

The problem is that many of our human highways cut across the paths that deer have used for generations. By following these well-worn routes, deer come right up to roadways, and must cross them to continue on their way.

Besides driving slowly and alertly in areas where deer are known to cross roads, people are trying to invent devices that will warn the deer away from the roadways in the first place. Deer whistles are an example. Mounted on the front fender of a car, these little devices are supposed to emit a high-pitched whistle that will frighten the deer and make it jump out of the roadway. The problem is, says John McDonald, deer can't hear the whistle. Their hearing falls within the same range as ours—so if we can't hear a sound, they can't either.

A device that does have promise in keeping deer off roads is the Strieter-Lite highway reflector. It's a specially designed plastic prism mounted on a post that reflects the headlights of oncoming cars across the road into the woods where the deer are. Because the lights aren't constantly shining and because they glow more brightly as the car approaches, the deer don't get used to them, ex- plains John Strieter, the Strieter-Lite's inventor. These reflectors have been used successfully in British Columbia, Canada (where they've also been found to work with elk and moose) and in several American states. Currently, a number of researchers are studying the Strieter-Lite's effectiveness, hoping to find statistical evidence that the devices work. Right now, things are looking promising, as stretches of highway that had been the site of as many as seventy accidents in past years now experience no deer-car collisions at all.

No guns allowed

In addition to the increase in the deer population and the movement of people into areas that had been forest and meadow, there is another reason for the abundance of deer. Simply put, there's no hunting allowed in cities and suburban areas. Most communities don't allow guns to be fired near houses or roads.

Why? Because people can easily get hurt or killed if the person wielding the gun doesn't know what he's doing. Many of today's high-caliber guns can fire ammunition at such a velocity that the bullet can pass right through the walls of a house. In addition, stray bullets can travel for a mile or more before they run out of steam—and anyone or anything in the bullet's way will be wounded. To eliminate that risk, communities don't allow weapons to be fired within their limits, except by police officers. Landowners can allow hunters to hunt on their private property, but the rules still apply: the weapon can't be fired within 500 feet of a house or 150 feet of a road.

Hunting is the most controversial solution to any conflict between humans and deer. Steve Lewis, of the Minnesota office of the U.S. Fish and Wildlife Service, and his colleagues had to find a way to handle the overabundance of deer in the Minnesota Valley National Wildlife Refuge, which borders four cities and stretches thirty-two miles along the Minnesota River. Everyone from city officials to hunters to animal-rights activists were involved, and the Fish and Wildlife people knew there would be conflict. With the help of a facilitator (who kept people from getting carried away and calling each other names), the group spent eighteen months working to find a solution. In the end, a weekend hunt in the park was allowed, with the following conditions:

- only a select few hunters were allowed to take part;

- they could hunt only in specified areas of the refuge;

- they could use only shotguns (which, because of their lesser range, require hunters to get closer to the deer than rifles do);

- hunters could shoot only does, not bucks, because the hunt's focus was to control the population, not get trophies for the hunters.

Many people object to the use of lethal methods to "solve" a human-wildlife conflict. Although it may seem like the easiest solution, it is not a final one; if you kill all the deer in one area, chances are good that deer will soon move in from other places to take over the vacant habitat. There's an old saying, "Nature abhors a vacuum," and it certainly applies here. Hunting is best saved for a last-ditch solution, when nothing else works.

What to do?

Resolving the conflict between people and whitetails isn't easy. What should our responsibility be? Deer are thriving in our suburbs because we provide them with plenty of good things to eat and protection from predators. In such ideal habitat, deer reproduce quickly. On average, according to John McDonald, a doe will have 1.2 fawns a year (that means some does have a single fawn while others have twins). That means in Massachusetts alone, 50,000 does can give birth to 60,000 fawns every year.

If too many deer live in a habitat, they can strip the vegetation bare, even ripping bark off the trees as high as they can reach. In wilderness areas, situations like this can lead to starvation, especially in the winter. Overpopulation can also lead to the spread of diseases and parasites, such as stomach worms and lung worms, explains wildlife veterinarian Victor Nettles, director of the Southeast Cooperative Wildlife Disease Study at the College of Veterinary Medicine at the University of Georgia. Without some system of checks and balances, population growth can lead to disaster, what scientists call a population crash. In a crash, a large number of animals die suddenly.

In addition, notes Steve Lewis, deer can also damage the habitats they live in by over-eating particular kinds of plants. For example, in the Minnesota Valley Wildlife Refuge, the deer tend to eat the native oaks and other native plants but leave imported species such as buckthorn and prickly ash alone. Unchecked, these imported species can spread quickly into the areas where the native plants used to be, crowding them out of the forest understory.

So if we don't want to hunt the deer, yet we don't want them to die possibly agonizing deaths from disease and starvation, what can we do?

The alternative that seems to have the best potential for slowing down the deer population's growth without turning to hunting is developing birth control for deer. According to deer expert Lee Fitzhugh of the University of California at Davis, the drawback to the deer birth control medication now available is that it must be given twice each year for it to be effective. And since deer look so much alike (to us, anyway), it's just about impossible to tell which does have gotten their birth-control shots and which ones haven't.

However, on Fire Island in New York, deer birth control is working pretty well. The program, run by the Humane Society of the United States, has cut down on the number of fawns born each year to the area's 200 deer. Each doe gets a dose of contraceptive delivered by a dart from a blowgun.

A form of birth control that will be effective with just one dose needs to be developed for this solution to work, and scientists at the Humane Society of the United States are trying to develop one. But it will still take time and expense to administer the medication to the deer.

Communities argue about how best to handle the situation. North Haven, New York, a town on Long Island, has a large deer population. Deciding how to manage the deer has torn the town apart, pitting neighbors against each other. One resident who asked for permission to hunt deer on his property was sued by a neighbor for a million dollars.

Some of the town's residents see the deer as pets, and provide them with apples, grain, and other food. Other residents see them as pests. Frank Brehmer has lived in North Haven since 1971. He recalls that when he first moved in, "You couldn't see through the trees, the woods were so thick." But today, the deer have literally eaten away the forest understory. As far as gardening is concerned, "If you want anything to grow, you need to protect it with an eight-foot fence," Brehmer explains. "And that's not a very attractive solution."

Over the past several years, North Haven residents have tried fences, unpalatable plants (which the deer have eaten anyway) and even considered bringing in sharpshooters to kill the deer (this idea was voted down). They've tried birth control, but found the time and costs involved prohibitive. For now, they are living with their deer, and property owners who find the deer too much of a nuisance are able to obtain a permit to bring bow hunters on their property to kill the deer. But the deer come right back. Brehmer notes that over the last three years, six hundred deer have been killed, "and you wouldn't notice the difference."

As the residents of North Haven have discovered, there is no easy answer when deer are involved.

5. Disease Concerns

Wild animals face the threat of disease, and some illnesses can be passed to humans.

In 1992, disaster struck the wild raccoons of Massachusetts. It was not a forest fire, or a flood, or a new type of gun. In fact, it wasn't even something that could be seen. But it decimated the raccoon population, killing most of the state's wild raccoons over just a few months.

That something was rabies.

Rabies is a dreaded disease, sometimes called hydrophobia, that is caused by a virus. The virus invades the nervous system of mammals. For a wild creature, rabies is a death sentence. Even for a domestic animal or for a human, rabies is fatal unless it is treated before the virus reaches the nervous system and symptoms appear.

Innocent victims: Rabies has taken a huge toll among raccoons in the East. Photo by Nell Baldacchio, courtesy of the U. S. Fish and Wildlife Service

Rabies has long been feared. It was mentioned as long ago as 23 B.C. in Egyptian writings, making it the oldest recorded infection in human history.

Rabies is generally spread through contact with an infected animal's saliva. If a raccoon is attacked by a rabid raccoon and bitten, the rabies virus enters the healthy raccoon's body through the bite. However, the illness may not show itself immediately; the rabies virus can be present in an animal for as long as a year or as little as a week. The difference in times depends on how near the bite has placed the virus to the nerve endings. If the bite has embedded the virus in muscle, it may take quite a while for the virus to move to the nerves. Yet if the bite has placed the virus near or on the nerves, the virus will spread quickly, traveling along the nerves to the spinal cord and brain, and from there to the digestive and respiratory systems and the salivary glands. From the salivary

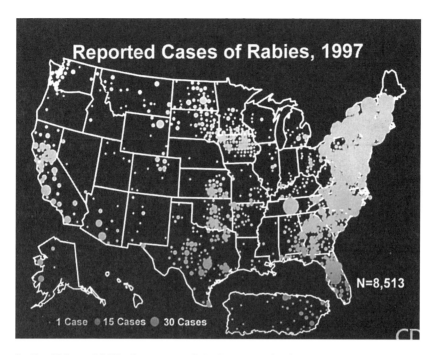

Reported Cases of Rabies, 1997

N=8,513

1 Case 15 Cases 30 Cases

In the U.S. in 1997, there were 8,513 cases of rabies reported in animals. Most were in wild animals; and only four cases were reported in humans. As you can see by this map, rabies is most common in the eastern part of the country. Courtesy of the Centers for Disease Control

glands, it can be passed to the next animal (or person) the infected animal bites.

Rabies has two forms: furious rabies and dumb rabies. In the furious form, an animal will foam at the mouth and act very aggressively. Most people who see these signs are sensible enough to stay away—after all, a dog foaming at the mouth is a terrifying sight. The second form, dumb rabies, isn't as frightening because the animal isn't "mad" or aggressive: people will often make the mistake of picking up an apparently tame animal. But the simple fact that a wild animal will let you come near it is a warning you shouldn't ignore—NEVER pick up a wild animal!

Rabies is found throughout the world except for Australia and Antarctica. In North America, raccoons are major carriers of rabies, particularly in the eastern United States. Skunks are the major carrier of rabies in the Midwest. Bats, foxes, and even woodchucks have been known to carry the disease. Rabies is a disease that affects only mammals. Besides these wild animals, it can also infect pet dogs and cats, horses, mules, sheep, cattle, and people.

Without treatment, an animal infected with rabies is sure to die. In 1996, 7,124 cases of rabies in animals were diagnosed in the United States. Of those, 6,550 were found in wild animals, and only 574 among domestic animals. Also in that year, four people died from rabies, one each in New Hampshire, Florida, Kentucky, and Montana.

Immunizing pets has lessened human exposure to rabies. In the early part of the twentieth century, if your dog got into a fight with an infected raccoon or fox, he'd bring the disease home to you. But with the development of the first rabies vaccine for dogs back in the 1950s, the chances of that have lessened dramatically. In 1955, 65 percent of the animal rabies cases reported to the U.S. Public Health Service were in domestic animals; of that number, 44 percent were dogs. During the 1950s, 113 people contracted rabies—most of them (seventy-one) through contact with a domestic animal—either a dog, a cat, or a cow. However, during the thirty years that followed the rabies vaccine's development, fifty-one Americans developed rabies, and of that number only twenty-three got it from a domestic animal (and fourteen of those bites had actually happened outside of the U.S.) According to Laura Simon of the Fund for Animals, no human cases of rabies have developed as a result of a raccoon bite.

In response to the rabies epizootic (the term scientists use for an epidemic among animals), many states passed laws requiring that all pet dogs and—for the first time—pet cats be vaccinated against rabies. It's especially important to immunize cats because some people still let them out at night, when they are more likely to run into wild animals than during the daytime. Most pet care experts advise that cat owners get their cats immunized and keep them inside, for safety's sake.

Some researchers have also looked into the possibility of vaccinating wild animals against the disease. Tests by veterinarians and biologists from Cornell University found that hiding an oral rabies vaccine in flavored bait can immunize raccoons against rabies; vaccine-laced baits (cookie-sized and made of marshmallow-flavored sugar, food-grade wax and fat) have helped control rabies in the red foxes living in Europe and southern Canada.

Rabies is a disease that been with us for centuries. Two other diseases have been recognized recently that can also be transferred from animals to people and/or their pets. These are Lyme disease and hantavirus.

Lyme disease

Lyme disease is named for the town of Lyme, Connecticut, where it was first recognized in 1975. It's caused by bacteria that are spread through the bite of certain ticks. In the northeast United States, Lyme disease is spread by deer ticks; in other parts of the country, it's spread by the deer tick's relatives, all in the scientific family *Ixodes*. The tick that transmits Lyme disease is smaller than a sesame seed.

Because these ticks depend on large animals—usually deer—to complete part of their life cycle, the greater the number of deer means the greater the number of ticks. Areas that have large deer populations also have large tick populations. In Wenham, Massachusetts, for example, the deer officer Steven Kavenaugh discourages people from walking in the woods during the spring because the risk of picking up a tick is so high. Kavenaugh has had Lyme disease himself, and knows many other people, including a town police officer, who suffer from it.

The adult ticks live and mate on large animals, like deer, during the fall and early spring. The female tick drops off the deer when the time comes to lay her eggs in the spring, and the eggs hatch into larva in the summer. The larva spend their summer living off the blood of small mammals, like mice, and then go dormant through the winter. In the next spring, they molt and become nymphs. The nymphs molt into adults in the fall and find large hosts to live on for the winter.

The nymph form of the tick is the one that usually passes the disease to people. However, the tick can pick up the bacteria that cause the disease at any stage in the life cycle, if it feeds on an infected animal, especially the white-footed mouse. Once infected, the tick will pass the disease on to any host it bites, whether mouse, bird, deer, or person.

Lyme disease is most common in New England, New York, New Jersey, Pennsylvania, Maryland, Minnesota, and Wisconsin, where there are 1.41 or more reported cases per 100,000 people (according to 1996 figures from the Centers for Disease Control and Prevention). Very few cases (0.00-0.08 cases per 100,000 people) have been reported in Alaska, Hawaii, Montana, South Dakota, Arizona, Utah, New Mexico, Colorado, Illinois, and Georgia. Lyme disease is the most common tick-borne disease in the country.

But just a single bite isn't enough for the disease to pass from tick to person: the nymph needs to be attached for about twenty-four hours for the bacteria that causes the disease to be passed, and adult ticks need to be attached for even longer, about thirty-six hours.

Kids, especially those under age ten, seem to be more likely to get Lyme disease than older people. It may be because they play outside more than teenagers or adults, and so are easy targets for the ticks. Young kids may also not notice attached ticks. They may also pick up the ticks more readily if the ticks ride in on family pets. However, there's no proof that people who own pets are more likely to get the disease than people who don't.

Lyme disease is difficult for doctors to diagnose because its symptoms are similar to those of so many other ailments. Even the most distinctive symptom—a red rash shaped like a bull's-eye—doesn't appear in every single case. Some people mistake their symptoms for a cold or the flu. Others get earaches. Some get sore throats, while others get headaches, suffer from nausea, or have jaw pain that's so severe they have trouble chewing. Even the rash isn't proof positive, because it can look like other skin ailments, such as hives or eczema. The only way to be certain about Lyme disease is to be tested, and the most effective way to be tested is to undergo two screening tests that look for anti-bodies in the blood, the ELISA test and the Immunoblotting, or Western Blot, test.

If Lyme disease goes undiagnosed and untreated, it can lead to arthritis, a painful swelling of the joints that can lead to deformity in severe cases. It can also affect the heart, skin, and nervous system.

A vaccine against Lyme disease became available in late 1998. Called LYMErix, it has promise, but like all vaccines isn't foolproof. It hasn't been approved for use in kids under fifteen years of age or people over seventy, and three shots are necessary to get the full effect—and when the vaccine was in-troduced, the shots had to be administered over the course of a year.

As they do with many new vaccines, people have mixed reac-tions. Some are getting the shots now; others, like Steven Kave-naugh, have decided to wait a while and see what kind of side effects the vaccine causes. In either case, people should be sure to follow these steps to cut down on their risk:

The deer mouse spreads hantavirus through its urine and droppings, although it seems unaffected by the disease itself. Courtesy of the Centers for Disease Control

- wear light-colored clothing when outside (which makes the tick nymphs easier to see);

- wear long sleeves and long pants;

- tuck the cuffs of your pants into your socks, which will keep the ticks from crawling up your pant legs and attaching to your skin;

- check your skin thoroughly for any signs of ticks when you get home.

Hantavirus

Although Lyme disease has been recognized just recently, hantavirus is an even more recent entrant in the annals of American medicine. It was first recognized in the U.S. in 1993, although hantaviruses have been causing illness in Europe and Asia for decades.

The strain, or variety, of hantavirus discovered in 1993 is called the Sin Nombre virus. Unlike other hantaviruses, which attack the kidneys, it attacks the lungs, causing an illness called hantavirus pulmonary syndrome, or HPS. Health authorities first became aware of this virus when a young Navajo man, suffering from shortness of breath, died shortly after arriving at a New Mexico hospital. His fiancee had died a few days earlier after a similar illness. Within a couple of months, fast-working researchers discovered that their illness was caused by a new strain of hantavirus—the Sin Nombre virus.

Hantaviruses are passed from rodents, especially deer mice, cotton rats, rice rats, and white-footed mice, to humans. Very rarely, the virus is passed through a bite. In most cases, the person has been cleaning out an area where the mice or rats have nested. As the person sweeps or vacuums, tiny particles of rodent saliva, droppings, or urine float into the air, tossed there by the motion of the cleaning. Called "aerosols," these airborne particles—and the viruses they contain—can easily be inhaled. They lodge themselves in the lungs. The first signs of illness don't appear immediately; instead, it takes one to six weeks for the flu-like symptoms of muscle aches and fever to show up. These symptoms are soon followed by coughing and shortness of breath. At that point, the person must get to the hospital very soon, or he may die within hours.

Cases of HPS have occurred in twenty-four states, a total of just 137 in all. Most cases have been in New Mexico (forty-one) and Arizona (twenty-four).

The Andes virus, another strain of hantavirus related to the Sin Nombre virus, caused an HPS outbreak in Argentina that involved eighteen people. A team of researchers from the Centers for Disease Control helped Argentinean doctors study the outbreak, which happened between September 22 and December 5, 1996. Because of the low population of rodents in the area and the way the disease spread, the CDC scientists suspect that the Andes hantavirus may have been passed from person to person, according to an article in *Emerging Infectious Diseases* (April–June, 1997). However, the article's authors noted that more research needs to be done before any conclusions are drawn.

Plague

Perhaps you've chanted this nursery rhyme on the playground:

> *Ring around the rosie*
> *Pockets full of posies*
> *A-choos, a-choos*
> *We all fall down.*

That innocent rhyme has its roots in one of the most infamous of all diseases that can be passed from animals to humans: plague.

During the 1300s, epidemics of plague swept through Europe, killing 25 million people, about one-third of the entire population at the time. Although physicians then were helpless to understand how the disease spread or to treat it, we now know that rat fleas passed to humans the bacteria that caused the disease.

In this rhyme, "Ring around the rosie" describes the appearance of a flea bite. The second line comes from the folk remedy of carrying about posies, or flowers, to ward off the illness. "A-choos" are sneezes, a common symptom. And the last line represents all the people who died from the plague.

The disease is caused by a kind of bacteria called *Yersinia pestis*. It's found in rodents and their fleas. Mice, rats, chipmunks, ground squirrels, and prairie dogs all have been known to carry it. If too many of these rodent hosts die, the fleas will seek out new hosts. In settled areas, the new hosts can be people.

While rodents are the usual carriers of the plague in the United States, other animals can catch it from them. If a human being handles an animal that has plague, it's possible for the person to catch it, too. One college student found a bobcat that had been killed by a car, and decided to skin the animal and make a rug for his dorm room. The bobcat had plague, and the young man caught the disease. Fortunately, he was treated with antibiotics and recovered.

Although no plague outbreaks have neared the destructiveness of the Black Death of the 1300s, people have died of the disease as recently as 1994, when plague broke out in Surat, India. Fifty-four people died, but hundreds more were saved by timely doses of antibiotics.

If you encounter a dead wild animal, steer clear: it may have been the host of plague-carrying fleas that are looking for a new place to live. And you don't want that to be you!

Other diseases to be aware of

Another disease that can be passed from animals to humans is giardiasis.

In the United States, giardiasis is the most common human disease caused by parasites. It is sometimes called "Beaver Fever," and that's not really fair to the beavers. For many years, it was believed that this parasitic organism was passed to people from beavers when the beavers defecated in the water supply and people drank the water. Recent studies have shown that isn't necessarily the case.

Giardiasis is caused by a parasitic protozoan called *Giardia lamblia*. It infests the small intestine and causes serious diarrhea about three weeks after the organism is first swallowed. People can remained infected for years.

The parasite is usually passed through water that's been contaminated with animal or human wastes. The major sources of the disease are now considered to be sheep and cattle, not beavers.

If you're out hiking, be sure to purify any stream water before drinking it by using a purifying filter, iodine tablets, or boiling the water for at least three minutes to protect yourself from giardiasis.

Similarly, the presence of a large number of animals, such as Canada geese, on a lake or pond can introduce illness-causing bacteria into the water. The animals' feces can contain a kind of bacteria called *Escherichia coli*, or *E. coli*. *E. coli* can cause fever and diarrhea if a person drinks water that is contaminated with it, whether the person drinks it deliberately or swallows water accidentally while swimming. This is not the usual way a person picks up an *E. coli* infection; most often such infections come from poor hygiene (such a person changing a baby's diaper or using the toilet and not washing his or her hands) or from eating undercooked beef, according to the Centers for Disease Control. However, the possibility for infection is present, so be sure to avoid swallowing pond water, and to drink only treated, purified water.

A new development that has health officials worried is the appearance of the West Nile virus. The virus had never been found in North America before 1999, when wildlife officials noticed the deaths of hundreds of birds, especially crows. When they studied the birds, they found damage to their brains.

In late November 1999, researchers at the National Wildlife Health Center, part of the U.S. Geological Survey, reported that the virus had been found in eighteen species of birds, including bald eagles, blue jays, and crows, in New York, Connecticut, Maryland, Pennsylvania, and New Jersey.

Why are health officials concerned about a virus in birds? They're worried because the virus can be transmitted from birds to humans by mosquitoes. A mosquito bites an infected bird and picks up the virus. When the mosquito bites a person, it passes the virus into the person's bloodstream. The virus killed seven people in the New York City area in early 1999. Most at risk are young children, elderly people, and people who have problems with their immune systems. While healthy adults experience mild, flu-like symptoms for several days, the people in this high-risk group develop encephalitis, which is an inflammation of the brain. It can lead to coma and even death.

Health and wildlife officials are concerned that birds could spread the virus when they fly south. They have sprayed areas where mosquitoes live with pesticides to try and stop the spread of the virus. Only time will show if they have been successful.

From reading these descriptions, you might be so worried about catching a disease from a wild animal that you're afraid to step out your back door! But you don't have to be. It's okay—and good—to get out and enjoy nature, and admire the wild neighbors that pass through your area. What you need to do to protect yourself is use common sense.

If you've been outside in the tall grass, make sure to check your skin for any signs of ticks. If you find one, have an adult remove it carefully. The adult should use pointed tweezers to grasp the tick behind the head and pull it backwards and out. It's important to make sure to get the whole tick out; sometimes people accidentally remove just the body and leave the head in. If you live in an area where Lyme disease is common, save the tick in rubbing alcohol or tape it to an index card; this will help the doctor identify what kind of tick it is in case you start showing some of the symptoms of Lyme disease.

To protect yourself from rabies, *never* go near a wild animal that's acting peculiar, either too aggressive or too friendly. If you find an injured wild animal, get an adult to help you, and contact your local dog officer, wildlife rehabilitator, or animal rescue society.

Be careful when cleaning out areas where there might be mice or rats, to avoid hantavirus. If you come upon a dead animal, don't pick it up, and don't drink untreated, unpurified water.

Remember, the part of your body that will do the most to keep you healthy in situations like these is your brain.

6. Predators Among Us

Humans have been at war with other predators for centuries. Can we learn to live with them?

When spotting a deer in the backyard, a person may feel awe, or, if his roses have been nibbled once too often, annoyance. Geese and beavers may also cause mixed emotions, depending on a person's experience with the animals.

But when a person sees a coyote under the forsythia bush, or a bear in the dumpster, the reaction can be very different. Rather than awe or annoyance, many people feel a more basic emotion: fear.

Like geese, deer, and the other creatures we've discussed, predators are making a comeback in suburban areas. Coyotes and foxes are a relatively common sight. Black bears frequent dumpsters and landfills (and one almost crashed a college party in Connecticut). Rumors of wolves circulate in northern New England, and wolves are a reality in Wisconsin and Minnesota. Even North America's wild cats seem to be returning to areas where they haven't been seen in hundreds of years (although biologists are still debating whether they're really there or not, just as they are about the wolves). But unlike other species of animals that are sharing our space, these animals make us afraid.

Fearing predators goes back to our beginnings. In the early days of human evolution, we were easy prey for a prehistoric cat or dire wolf. Stripped of a gun to fire or a truck or building to hide in, modern human beings aren't able to put up much of a fight against nature's predators. We have stubby little teeth, we lack claws, and we can't run all that fast. But we do have something that will help us deal with the presence of predators among us: We have brains. And with common sense and logic, we can most likely live in a tolerant atmosphere with the creatures that in the past we've devoted so much time and effort to wiping out.

What is a predator, anyway?

If someone asked you to describe a predator, what would you say? Would you say it has sharp teeth? Claws? Or maybe you think of a bird of prey when you hear the word "predator" and into your mind comes a picture of curved talons and a hooked beak.

Simply put, a predator is an animal that eats other animals to survive. It doesn't have to be a shark or a lion. For instance, the American robin is a predator. It feeds mainly on earthworms. In fact, most of our songbirds are predators, each consuming thousands of bugs a year.

Insects themselves are tremendous predators. Not only are there insects that eat other insects, like dragonflies and praying mantises, but some insects can even eat vertebrate animals—like the species of water bug that especially likes to eat tadpoles.

Spiders are famous predators. They eat mostly insects, too, but some large spiders can catch and eat birds.

Snakes are also famous predators. They eat eggs, mice, rats, birds, and even other snakes. The biggest snake, the anaconda, can capture and eat wild pigs called peccaries, and even small crocodiles.

Even the simple sea star is a predator. Scallops snap their shells open and shut rapidly to move away from one. The sea star is about as far from the picture of a sharp-toothed predator that you can imagine. Not only does it have no teeth, it doesn't even have a head.

Unfortunately, most people don't think that the robin on their lawn or the ladybug on their finger is just as much a predator as any wolf or cougar. They tend to think of the big mammalian predators (like wolves), and they think none too kindly of them to boot.

The longest war

For centuries, people have been concentrating on wiping out predators wherever and whenever possible. Not only do we tell scary stories about predators (remember Little Red Riding Hood?), but we act on our fear by killing the creatures we are so afraid of.

For example, take humankind's relationship with the wolf. Historically, wolves lived all over the world, including Europe and Asia—areas that were populated by people as well. And people killed wolves and their rulers encouraged it. In England in the tenth century, King Edward let his people pay their taxes in wolf heads. By the 1700s, no wolves roamed the British Isles, and they had been beaten back in most of the rest of Europe.

When early explorers and settlers arrived in North America, they found the wolf here, too. Approximately a quarter of a million wolves hunted deer, elk, moose, and other prey, raised their pups, and lived in packs that are truly marvels of social organization. But the early European colonists weren't the least bit interested in learning about these animals: they wanted them gone.

By 1630, Massachusetts had already established a bounty on the wolf, the sum of one penny per wolf. Ten years later, the bounty was 40 shillings. The colony even encouraged Native Americans to take part in the wolf's extermination by promising a bounty of corn or wine for each dead wolf a native hunter brought in. New Jersey established a wolf bounty in 1697 of 20 shillings (about $2.50).

Through hunting, killing the wolves' natural prey animals (especially deer), and clearing the forest for farmland, colonists did away with the wolf in the East. By 1800, few wolves remained in New England, and the last one was killed in Maine in 1860. Wolves hung on in upstate New York and parts of Pennsylvania until around 1900, but then they too, were gone.

However, wolves and their smaller cousins the coyotes still lived in the West. As had happened in the East, humans killed off their natural prey—particularly the bison—so the wolves turned to hunting livestock.

Compared to deer, bison, elk, or other wild prey, domestic animals are easy to catch. They aren't real speedsters, nor do they have the "street smarts" that wild hoofed animals do. And for a predator, an easy catch is a good one, especially if the predator is old, sick, or crippled by injury.

Hunting takes a lot of energy, and that energy is wasted if the hunt isn't a success. An alert, healthy deer is as likely to get away from a predator as it is to be caught (unless something works in the predator's favor, such as deep snow or the element of surprise). So when presented with the chance to kill something that's easy to catch, like a sheep, it's no wonder why some predators will take the opportunity.

However, the people raising the livestock didn't see it that way (and still don't). Every sheep or steer killed by predators meant money out of their own pockets because they had already invested lots of time and money in buying, raising and taking care of the stock. Having an animal killed on the range by a predator rather than having it make it to market meant a loss of investment and of income. (In North Dakota, an outlaw wolf called "Three Toes" killed $50,000 worth of livestock back in the 1920s before a wolf trapper got him.)

So with the American government's okay, the western ranchers continued the war on predators that the colonists in the East had started. The war didn't stop with wolves: Any creature that might possibly be suspected of killing cattle or sheep was a target. Sheep ranchers shot bald and golden eagles out of the sky because it was believed they killed lambs. Cougars, which prey mostly on deer, were shot whenever they were seen, as were grizzly bears, although we now know their diet is made up of a lot of plant matter, fish, and some meat.

Throughout the 1800s, guns, traps, and poisons killed millions of predators, including hawks, eagles, bobcats, foxes, lynxes, coyotes, wolves, cougars, black bears, and grizzlies.

Understanding the predator's role

Again, we learned nearly too late what a mistake our actions were. Predators play a vital role in a healthy ecosystem. They are the ultimate source of population control on other animals.

As we saw in an earlier chapter, without the wolves and cougars, there's nothing to stop deer from reproducing (and reproducing, and reproducing!). Animals that enjoy a high reproductive rate produce a lot of offspring—remember the example of the Canada geese on the soccer field and their hundreds of descendants in just a few years? In nature, a habitat usually can't handle having so many deer or geese. They can strip grassy areas bare and leave trees leafless. And then there is no more food. What happens next?

Sometimes they'll move on. But more often, they'll stay. They get skinnier and skinnier, and fall victim to all kinds of ailments. Some will even starve to death.

Predators, by killing both adult and young prey animals, keep the population from getting so out of hand. By maintaining the number of animals at a number the habitat can support, predators help make sure there's enough for everyone—predator and prey alike.

The big three, plus one

If you're a predator, size rules. That means the larger you are, the higher you are on the ladder that is the relationship of North American predators.

On the lower rungs are the small predators, like foxes, raccoons, and skunks. On the rung above these animals are the medium-sized predators, such as the bobcat and the coyote, whose arrival in the eastern suburbs has shaken up the orderly existence the smaller predators had enjoyed for so long. At the top of the ladder are the major predators: the cougar, the wolf, and, on the loftiest rung, the bear.

Members of the "Big Three" are rarely seen in the suburbs, especially the wolf and the cougar because of their restricted ranges. However, just because we haven't seen them doesn't mean they aren't there. In 1996, scientists discovered a female wolf spending more than a week in the suburbs of Minneapolis and St. Paul, Minnesota. They realized she was there only because she was wearing a radio collar, put on her by researchers in Wisconsin. The

When this cub wandered into the suburbs with its mother and sibling, they were tranquilized and taken to a wooded area of the state. Some- times such interlopers are shot as nuisances, or out of fear. Photo by Rick Hartford/*The Hartford Courant*

collar broadcast a signal that researchers picked up. After ten days, the wolf moved on. Without the radio collar, no one would have known she was there, notes Mike Don Carlos of the Min- nesota Department of Natural Resources. If one wolf can do this, it's possible that other large predators might be visiting our neigh- borhoods too.

One predator that people are seeing more of in the suburbs is the black bear (*Ursus americanus*). The black bear population is growing fast and more bears means more encounters between bears and people.

Residents of West Haven, Connecticut, got quite a surprise in the spring of 1999. A young black bear wandered into town, trav- eling through some neighborhoods and almost crashing a party at the University of New Haven. The bear neared one of the state'sbusiest intersections during the night, until local police officers managed to herd it away from the road and shoo it up a tree. State wildlife officials tranquilized the bear the next morning and took it out of the city and back to the northwest part of the state, where most of Connecticut's fifty or so black bears live.

Judging by the tags on the 200-pound male bear, he had also been in New York and Massachusetts. His visit to West Haven—on the shores of Long Island Sound—marked the southernmost point for a black bear in the state's recent history. Only a year before, a black bear was sighted several times in Cheshire, just twenty miles to the north.

State wildlife biologist Paul Rego said the bear probably has been around people quite a bit. "He's used to them," he told a reporter for the *New Haven Register* after the incident.

Humans and bears are encountering each other more and more often. Bears have learned that people provide great sources of food in the form of their orchards, landfills, cornfields, dumpsters, and bird feeders. According to James E. Cardoza, black bear project leader for the Massachusetts Department of Fisheries and Wildlife, bears have good memories, and so when the foods they naturally eat in the forest run low, they remember where they've found food before and go back there.

Bears, even the relatively small black bear, can frighten people when they show up where they aren't expected—in the backyard, for instance. Robert Engle, a biology professor at Marlboro College in Vermont, remembers when a black bear appeared in his backyard. Engle and his wife stood stock-still as the bear passed several yards from them. When his wife turned her head, the bear spotted the motion and stopped dead. After a few moments, he retreated back into the trees.

Why didn't the bear notice the Engles until she moved? Like many predators, bears have eyesight that is more attuned to movement than to color. By holding still, the Engles didn't attract the bear's attention. People who encounter a bear in their yard need to stay calm, hold still, and move slowly away. Although black bears are generally harmless to people, they have occasionally killed people, including a four-year-old boy in Canada in 1994.

However, we're actually doing more damage to the bears than they are to us. Bears that grow to depend on human trash at dumpsters and landfills rarely survive very long after those food sources are removed. It's as though they forget how to find food on their own. And yet when we find them in our trash or under a house, we usually shoot and kill them.

Mammoth Lakes, California, is a resort town twenty-seven miles from Yosemite National Park that gets more than a million visitors a year who come to enjoy its skiing and natural beauty. Coexisting with the residents and all these tourists within the town's limits (it covers about sixteen square miles) are thirty to forty black bears.

Despite living close to people, no black bears have been shot as nuisances in Mammoth Lakes for years, thanks to the work of the town's own bear man, Steven Searles. For the last four years, Searles has made it his job (with the town's okay) to keep the bears from acting up. He responds to calls for help when a bear has taken up residence where he's not wanted, or has otherwise gotten out of line. Searles arrives and drives the bear away with scoldings and, sometimes ("if the bear's been naughty," says Searles), rubber bullets, pepper spray, or fireworks. Sometimes he needs his dog Tucker, a special breed from Finland, to harass the bear and drive it out of the area. Searles also uses body language and bearlike noises (such as "huffing") to tell the bears, in their own language, that they're out of line.

Searles describes his job as one of educating the animals about where the boundaries are—that is, what kind of behavior won't be tolerated. He makes it clear that he's not driving the bears out of the town, but rather away from the spot where they're getting into mischief.

The methods work. "It's rare that I work a bear more than once or twice," he says. The animals quickly learn where they aren't wanted. The bears aren't hurt and neither are the people, even in situations when it seems disaster could easily result. On Easter morning 1999, Searles evicted a bear from the base of one of the town's ski lifts, which was surrounded by hundreds of people.

More and more communities are becoming interested in Searles's success. The Sierra Nevada County Sheriff's Department is now using his way of dealing with bears. Canadian authorities are looking at his method too, as that country seeks an alternative to killing the bears: In 1998, Canadian authorities shot 4,500 black bears ("for getting into their trash," Searles says).

Searles has studied bears closely during the twenty-two years he's lived in the town. He himself used to hunt and trap. But when hunting and trapping declined in popularity, "I saw the potential to be with animals and help my community," he says. Although he still tries to teach people how to act around wild animals, he says it's easier to teach the animals how to behave around people.

And the bears are good students. Since he assumed the job of "Wildlife Research and Management Consultant," not a single bear has been shot as a "nuisance bear." And that makes him rightly proud.

Could Searles's method work elsewhere in the U.S.? There's no reason to think it shouldn't, since Searles has trained other people to do what he does. If we can use methods like Steven Searles's and better understand what draws bears to human farms and settlements in the first place, perhaps we can make our encounters with bears more an opportunity for wonder than for fear.

Clever and adaptable, the coyote is quickly becoming the top predator in the suburbs. Courtesy of the U.S. Fish and Wildlife Service

Enter the coyote

As you can see, your chances of running into a bear, wolf, or cougar in your backyard at this time are probably quite slim. However, their absence has actually encouraged the arrival of the coyote, a medium-sized predator that people in the eastern suburbs are seeing more and more frequently.

For years, we've had small predators living among us, such as raccoons and foxes. Never exterminated like their larger counterparts, they've kept a low profile and gone largely unnoticed—except, of course, when one of them has dined at the trash barrel and spread it around the yard. These small predators do us the service of keeping populations of mice and other creatures under control.

But every ecosystem, even the one in the suburbs, generally has a top predator—the one that rules the roost, as it were. Historically, the top predator was the wolf or the bear. Without them, that top spot was up for grabs—and the coyote (*Canis latrans*) is just the canine for the job.

Not as large as the wolf, the coyote stands about two feet tall at the shoulder and is about four feet long, including a bushy tail. Most coyotes weigh about forty pounds, although the ones now found in the eastern U.S. are bigger, weighing about sixty pounds. Glimpsed as it runs across a playing field or disappears into the trees, the coyote can easily be mistaken for a dog.

Quick and intelligent, coyotes are able and willing to make a meal out of just about anything. Although small mammals like mice, voles, and rabbits make up more than half of their diet, coyotes will also eat grasshoppers, berries, acorns, garden vegetables, sunflowers, road kills, pet food, and even domestic pets, like house cats and small dogs. (Many people consider the unexplained disappearance of pet cats to be the first sign that a coyote has moved into the neighborhood, although biologists shake their heads at this.)

Coyotes were first noticed in New York State way back in 1912, and Massachusetts farmers saw them during the 1930s. Since the

---

Warning: A coyote may look like a dog, but it isn't.

Although they may look doglike, it's important to remember that coyotes can't be approached like domestic dogs. They are wild animals, and will defend themselves. The injured coyote found in Boston snarled and snapped at the animal experts who came to capture her and bring her to a veterinary clinic for help. Any animal—even your pet dog or cat—can attack if hurt, in pain, and frightened.

1960s, they've picked up speed and spread even to thickly settled areas, such as New Jersey. One morning in 1998, startled Bostonians found an injured coyote huddled on the steps on one of that city's famous brownstones.

Although coyotes are just tourists on the streets of Boston, they've made themselves at home both in that city's suburbs and in other areas. Part of the reason for the coyote's presence (besides the lack of larger predators to deal with) is that the suburbs offer the coyote a smorgasbord of food to choose from. Look around at what people may have in their yards and gardens that will interest a hungry coyote, on just one typical street:

House #1 has a small vegetable garden out back

House #2 has pet rabbits in a hutch

House #3 doesn't have any lids for their garbage cans, and animals have no trouble tearing through the plastic trash bags

House #4 feeds the dog out on the back deck, and bowls of dry dog food and water are always available

House #5 also has a vegetable garden, and a bird feeder

House #6 has an open compost pile with lots of fresh peelings and discards

House #7 feeds the stray cats in the neighborhood by leaving cat food out all night

House #8 has a long row of sunflowers across the back of the property

Each one of these houses—including house #8—is providing something that the coyote will eat, whether it's fresh produce, pet food or garbage. Some people deliberately feed the coyotes, too, marvels biologist Susan Langlois of the Massachusetts Division of Fisheries and Wildlife. Besides encouraging them to come looking around our houses for food, this practice has another down side: It gets them used to people.

In North Dakota, coyotes are afraid of people, notes biologist Marsha Sovada of the Northern Prairie Wildlife Research Center in Jamestown, North Dakota, part of the U.S. Geological Survey. Western coyotes have grown up associating the appearance of a person with the *crack-tzing!* of a gunshot. Western coyotes know people mean trouble, and do all they can to avoid us. However, Eastern coyotes don't encounter people in such a situation that often. They don't know they should be afraid of us, and thus don't worry about coming onto our property and even up onto our steps in search of food. So it's up to humans to teach coyotes what the boundaries are, says Langlois. She says she likes to hear a person report sighting a coyote that has passed through his property on its way somewhere else. She's less pleased when someone calls complaining about a coyote lounging in his yard and admits that the coyote's been hanging around for weeks—and that the humans have done nothing to encourage it to move along.

"We've got to re-instill the fear coyotes have of humans," Langlois asserts. While she never suggests that people should chase after a coyote ("You've got to respect them for the medium-sized predator they are," she says), she encourages adults to use "negative reinforcement" to teach the coyotes the rules. Scare devices like those that work for deer, electric fencing, even shouting and waving your arms or squirting the hose at the coyote will "freak it out a little," she says, and show it that it isn't top dog—you are.

"Just because they exist doesn't mean they're going to be a problem," Langlois says. The coyotes are here to stay. Humans need to behave responsibly and not encourage the coyotes to behave in a way they'll get into serious trouble for later. That means not feeding them or providing them with easy food sources. Keep trash cans tightly lidded and keep pets indoors.

What should you do if you see a predator?

Overall, wildlife experts say your chances of encountering a big predator in a suburban backyard are small. In most such settings, you're more likely to see a coyote or fox, or perhaps even a bobcat. If you do, use common sense. If you are outside, don't run—movement attracts their attention, and if you run you may get chased. And don't run after the predator, either—that can result in your getting hurt.

Don't panic. Go inside. Keep your dog or cat inside with you and watch the predator from the safety of your living room or kitchen.

After all, we've encouraged other forms of wildlife to join us around our homes. It's only to be expected that the predators would come too.

Be tolerant and careful, and enjoy the fact that nature's heavy hitters are making a comeback.

7. Success Stories

With education and understanding, people can and do learn to appreciate and make room for the animals among us.

The bats weren't a welcome sight. The residents of Austin, Texas, were stunned when they learned that bats (Mexican free-tailed bats, to be exact) had taken up residence on a major bridge in their city. The Congress Avenue Bridge had just been rebuilt, and the new supports were close enough together to make a wonderful roosting site for the bats. More than half a million bats had already taken up residence, and more were moving in nearly every day.

The sight of the bats leaving their roosts for their nightly search for food was frightening, and the local newspapers printed such sensational headlines as "Bats Take a Bite out of Austin."

Austin residents were really scared. They began talking about having the bats killed.

A large part of the reason for their fear was the terrible reputation that bats have. Now, it's true that bats are one of the creatures in North America that harbor rabies. But the chances of a human being coming into contact with a rabid bat are extremely small—less than one-half of one percent of bats actually carries rabies, and such bats die quickly. Human encounters with rabid bats generally only happen if the human is foolish enough to pick up a sick bat that's on the ground. (Bats don't get aggressive when they have the disease, as some other mammals do.) But many people still believe the old false stories about bats, among them:

- Bats are blind.
- Bats will suck your blood.
- Bats will get tangled in your hair.
- Bats are flying mice, and just like mice carry all kinds of diseases.

There are a lot of superstitions about bats in North America and Europe, possibly because the bat species that live in these areas are small and rarely seen. In areas where there are flying foxes, large bats with wingspans up to six feet, bats aren't feared; in fact, they're as normal as birds are to the people who live in these places.

However, when the people of Austin heard about the bats, their first impulse was to get rid of them. They wanted to poison them.

Fortunately for the bats, all the negative news coverage they were getting came to the attention of a man who loves bats and has devoted his life to saving them. His name is Merlin Tuttle.

At the time, Dr. Tuttle was working as a researcher at the Milwaukee Public Museum in Wisconsin. For more than twenty-five years, he had been traveling all over the world photographing and studying bats. He used the photos and knowledge he gained to teach people that bats are beneficial animals that should be protected, not persecuted. He not only wrote articles for such magazines as *National Geographic* and *International Wildlife*, but he also visited people all over the world to talk about bats. For example, he visited the Pacific Ocean islands of Guam and American Samoa, where some species of flying fox faced extinction because they had been overhunted for food. Merlin Tuttle was helping to protect these bats in faraway places, so he decided to help the bats in Austin, too.

He was so committed to this idea that he took a huge step. He left his job at the museum in Milwaukee and moved to Austin with his conservation group, Bat Conservation International. BCI (which, at the time, consisted of Dr. Tuttle and a secretary) moved into offices at the University of Texas at Austin in 1986, and Dr. Tuttle set out to teach the city's residents about their bats.

Mexican free-tailed bats are found in the southern half of the United States, especially in Texas, Arizona, New Mexico, and Oklahoma. Cave-dwellers, they grow to about four inches in length, with wingspans of about a foot. And like all bats, they are not flying mice, nor are they even related to rodents. They're an entirely different kind of mammal, and the only one that has truly learned to fly. (Other mammals, like the "flying squirrel," don't really fly—they just glide from tree to tree.)

Mexican free-tails live in the world's largest communities of mammals, with as many as 20 million bats making up one colony in Bracken Cave in Texas. Nowhere near that many live on the Congress Avenue Bridge—but 1.5 million bats make it the largest urban bat colony in the world.

With patience and persistence, Dr. Tuttle and his BCI staff spread the word. They visited city officials and school kids. They showed them wondrous photographs of bats in flight. They told them that the bridge's colony of bats would eat 30,000 pounds of insects every night. They told them that bats weren't the nightmarish monsters that Hollywood movies made them out to be: rather, they are one of the world's most gentle and shy creatures.

It took a long time, almost ten years, for the people of Austin to get over their fear of bats. But today, the Congress Avenue Bridge's bat colony is one of Austin's top visitor attractions. The people of Austin come out at dusk to watch "their bats" take to the sky.

Without Dr. Tuttle's help, and the people's willingness to learn something new, the bats would be gone. Education turned a feared liability into an asset for Austin, and saved the life of the colony.

Bridges are not the only human-made structures that have appealed to wild creatures. In fact, the tall buildings of our cities may have actually helped in the recovery of one species from near extinction: the peregrine falcon.

Peregrines used to live throughout North America. But that was before humans came up with a new pesticide called DDT during the 1940s.

DDT was hailed as a miracle. Sprayed in large clouds, it killed mosquitoes by the millions, and stopped them from spreading malaria and other deadly diseases. But the miracle had a dark side.

After it was applied, DDT didn't just kill some bugs and then wash away with the rain. Instead, it stayed in the ground, to be swallowed by insects long after it was applied. DDT didn't kill these insects, but it did stay in their bodies until they were eaten by a bird. DDT then built up in the bird's body over time and caused it harm.

Let's say that each insect contained in its body just a tiny bit of DDT: say 1/1000th of an ounce. If a bird consumed 1,000 insects, it also consumed an ounce of DDT.

And now let's add the peregrine to the equation, eating four birds a week. That adds up to four ounces of DDT a week—or a pound a month! See how the small amount in each insect turns into a lot when it reaches the capstone species, the top predator?

The DDT didn't kill the peregrines outright. Instead, it affected their eggs. The eggshells were too thin. This led to two problems. One, the eggs couldn't maintain the right balance of moisture within the egg; the water inside evaporated right out through the thin shell, and the baby falcon inside died. Two, the eggs couldn't bear the weight of the mother bird, so when she went to brood them (that is, sit on them and keep them warm so they could hatch), she crushed them accidentally.

Throughout the 1950s and 1960s, many peregrines were unable to successfully raise new chicks. Without young birds to replace them, older birds died and the population dwindled.

The effect of DDT and other pesticides on the falcons and the rest of the environment didn't go completely unnoticed, however. Rachel Carson was a biologist who had written several popular books that showed people the wonders of the world around them. During the 1950s, she became concerned about what she had seen DDT do to nature, and as a result decided to write about it. In 1962, her book *Silent Spring* was published. It told the world about the terrible effect DDT was having on nature, including the falcons. Her book met great resistance from pesticide manufacturers, who claimed that she was merely a "hysterical woman." But the truth bore out her words: whatever DDT could touch, it could kill. Thanks in large part to *Silent Spring*, DDT was outlawed in 1972. Even though Rachel Carson died in 1964, her legacy continues through the ecology movement that her work began.

After 1972, DDT could no longer legally be applied to fields in the United States. However, it still existed in the environment, and thus still affected the falcons. Dr. Thomas J. Cade, an ornithologist and falconer, knew that the peregrines were rapidly heading towards extinction. He knew that steps needed to be taken. And he came up with a radical idea.

He borrowed peregrines that belonged to falconers in Alaska and Canada, birds that hadn't been contaminated with DDT. These birds became the basis of a captive breeding program for the peregrines.

In a captive breeding program, the birds are allowed to mate and lay their eggs, much as they would in the wild. But rather than leaving the eggs with the parents, Dr. Cade removed the eggs and placed them in incubators. The eggs developed well and hatched. Meanwhile, the parent falcons laid more eggs. Each egg was more precious than gold, and Dr. Cade needed to get as many eggs as possible.

The eggs were raised into young chicks, which were then released into the wild. The first releases during the 1970s didn't succeed: none of the birds survived. But Dr. Cade and his staff learned with every release.

In 1984, six gangly chicks, covered with fuzzy white down, arrived in Boston, Massachusetts, as part of Dr. Cade's falcon recovery project. Overseeing the Boston release was Dr. Thomas French, who heads the state's endangered species program.

At first, the residents of eastern Massachusetts weren't crazy about the idea of releasing raptors in the capital city. Some believed that the peregrines were being brought in to kill pigeons and complained that that wasn't fair. Others worried about the possibility of falcon attacks on people.

Dr. French and his team talked to many reporters to explain that the birds weren't brought in for pigeon control, and that they would have very little contact with people. Some people remained skeptical, but the project was able to move ahead.

Dr. French and his team put the young falcons in a "hacking box," a shelter with three wooden walls and a door made of metal bars, on a six-foot tall platform on the roof of a downtown office building. Their attendants named the four males (tiercels) Cairo, Rio, Dublin and Sidney. The other two falcons were females (called falcons); their names were Madrid and Aberdeen.

When at last the birds' flight feathers grew in, Dr. French removed the bars of the hacking box. The youngsters made short flights from one building to another, and back to the box. They learned about the wind and their wings, and how to swoop and to soar. Young falcons who are raised in the wild learn these things from their parents. But these six birds had to learn on their own. While it took them longer than it would have with older birds to learn from, they managed quite well.

Until August. That month, Cairo crashed into a plate-glass window, broke his neck, and died three days later. A week later, Sidney was hit and killed by a small airplane at an airport outside of Boston. The same day, Madrid got caught in the turbulent air caused by a passing jet at Logan International Airport and broke her wing. Although with veterinary care the wing healed, Madrid couldn't go back to the wild. Instead, she went back to Dr. Cade's facility to become part of the captive breeding program.

Although the 50 percent success rate doesn't seem very good, the results were encouraging enough for Dr. French to bring more falcons to the hacking box in 1985.

However, no one expected Dublin to return. At first he spent much of his time terrorizing the new falcons. He chased them and screamed at them, causing one to have a fatal accident.

A female peregrine falcon watches over her chicks in their nest atop a Boston office tower. Once on the Endangered Species List, the falcons have taken up residence in a number of North American cities. Photo by Craig Koppoe, courtesy of the U.S. Fish and Wildlife Service

One day, something amazing happened. Dublin landed on the platform. The humans watched tensely. If Dublin attacked the younger birds, they could do nothing to save them.

Then one of the tiercels stepped toward Dublin, lowered his head, and began to bob it up and down. He was begging food from Dublin, as a chick will do to a parent bird.

From then on, Dublin's attitude changed. He wasn't as aggressive toward them. It was as if he'd appointed himself their stepdad. The four young birds followed his example, and quickly picked up his skills in flying and hunting.

By the end of July, the last of the new falcons had left for good. But Dublin remained. And soon his presence attracted the attention of a female a year younger than he, who had been released in Canada. They became a mated pair.

Finding a place to nest in the city is a challenge. Most window ledges are sloped. Although the falcons could perch on a sloping window ledge just fine, if they laid an egg it would just roll off and fall to the street below. In addition, peregrines don't build their nests out of sticks, mud, and feathers, like many birds. Instead, they build what scientists call a "scrape," a bowl-shaped hollow in gravel. The gravel holds in the eggs and protects them from rolling off the cliffs where falcons usually nest.

So French and his team built a nesting box and filled it with just the right kind of gravel. Remarkably, the birds found it when they returned to the city the following year. Soon two eggs sat on the gravel in the box—the first wild falcon eggs laid in Massachusetts in decades.

In August 1999, everyone involved with the falcon restoration project had reason to celebrate. The federal government removed the peregrine from the endangered species list. Falcons now live in cities around the country, including New York City, Chicago, Minneapolis, Los Angeles, and San Francisco.

The story of the peregrine is not just a tribute to the people involved: it's a tribute to the falcons themselves. They were able to adjust to an environment wildly different from the one their ancestors lived in. In place of their ancestors' tall cliffs, they made excellent use of the skyscrapers of human cities. They learned to hunt the abundant starlings and other small birds they found there. Adaptability is an important part of any species' survival story. The peregrines have shown that they aren't just fast—they're flexible, too.

You may be thinking that you need to be a scientist to foster and protect wildlife, or that it's something that happens in other places. But believe it or not, you can turn your own backyard into a wildlife sanctuary.

The National Wildlife Federation has run the Backyard Wildlife Habitat program since 1973. Through the program, more than 25,000 people in the United States, Canada, Peru, Puerto Rico, and Switzerland have made their yards and gardens great places for wildlife. The program has been so successful, in fact, that the NWF has expanded it to include schoolyards, workplaces, and even entire communities.

The program's manager, Heather Carskaddan, explains that the yard should provide food, cover, water, and a place to raise young for wild creatures. There's a variety of ways to meet each of these needs:

> *Food:* Set up one or more bird feeders, including humming-bird feeders. Plant shrubs, trees and flowers that provide natural sources of food when they create berries or nuts, such as acorns.

> *Water:* A small manmade pond is a great source of water for wildlife, but you don't need to get so complicated. A small fountain, a birdbath, or even a shallow dish of water will do the job (remember to clean the dish or birdbath regularly).

> *Cover:* Wild creatures need places to hide whenever danger threatens. Stone walls provide shelter for creatures like mice and snakes, while birds and rabbits will take cover in bushes or tall grass.

> *A place to raise young:* Dead trees provide lots of nesting holes for birds and squirrels, and they can build their nests in live trees, too. You could also provide bird nesting boxes that you build yourself!

The program encourages people to look at the beauty of the plants native to their areas and use them in their landscaping. The advantage that native plants have over the ones you buy from seed catalogs is that they are used to the climate in your area and will take care of themselves.

Businesses are finding that they can save a lot of money by landscaping with native species—in some cases, a million dollars over a period of ten years. Take the case of CIGNA Corporation, a large insurance firm in Bloomfield, Connecticut, a suburb of Hartford. When the headquarters was first built, it was surrounded by two hundred acres of lawn that had to be watered, fertilized, sprayed and mowed regularly. Then the corporation learned about the NWF Workplace Habitats program. Today, those two hundred acres have been cut down to just ninety-one, and the rest has been turned into meadows and forests. The new landscaping has attracted wildlife ranging from butterflies to wild turkeys and deer. Not only do employees and neighbors now have a lovely place to walk, but the company itself is enjoying saving almost half a million dollars every year.

The whole town of Alpine, California, is certified wildlife habitat—it was the first Community Wildlife Habitat certified by the NWF. Maureen Austin came up with the idea. Her yard and garden had been certified as backyard and schoolyard habitats. When the town's business people saw them, with their abundance of songbirds, butterflies, and hummingbirds, they were excited at the idea of spreading the beauty throughout the town.

Some people were reluctant to take part at first, thinking that they would be required to attract wildlife they weren't comfortable with, such as skunks or raccoons, Austin recalls. "You have to overcome certain fears," she notes. "Not everyone wants to attract all kinds of wildlife, but if you can meet them on a level they're willing to work with, then it can work." She and other project leaders helped these people understand that butterflies and birds are wildlife too, and that they could plant bushes that would provide food for them.

Austin and the project team also made it plain to residents that they didn't need a large spread to create a habitat. One elderly woman created a certified habitat on her balcony by setting up bird feeders and nest boxes and providing plants for the butterflies.

Another town resident earned his Eagle Scout rank for helping create a schoolyard habitat. And each student at the town's four schools raised a painted lady butterfly; their butterflies were released simultaneously on May 1, 1998, the day Alpine received its certification—all 2,000 of them!

Projects like this are not only good for wildlife, but also for the people. They draw community residents closer together as they work on the project and maintain it.

If you would like to find out more about the NWF's habitat programs, you can write to the National Wildlife Federation, 8925 Leesburg Pike, Vienna, Virginia 22184-0001, or visit their web site at www.nwf.org.

8. Personal Responsibility

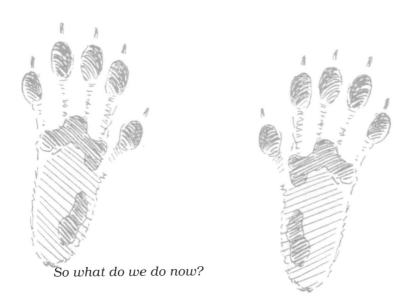

So what do we do now?

As the previous chapter made plain, animals don't always move into a human-dominated area on their own. They need the help of people who can provide education and some good public relations. We human beings aren't always willing to save an animal just because it plays a vital role in nature's system. The cute fuzzy ones, like the panda bear, or the noble ones, like the peregrine, are easy to love. It's the ugly ones, the scary ones, that face an uphill battle for our support.

Back in 1979, a young filmmaker named Steven Spielberg scared the pants off just about everyone in the United States when he released his movie *Jaws*. It was the story of a great white shark that terrorizes a seaside town, based on novel of the same name by Peter Benchley. But as much of a bestseller as Benchley's book had been, it had nowhere near the impact that the movie and its three mechanical man-eaters did.

People everywhere refused to go swimming in the ocean. Seaside resorts like the fictional one in the movie saw a huge downswing in the number of vacationers. But while tourists may have sweltered and merchants faced empty cash registers, the real losers were the sharks.

Sharks have always been feared by people. They appeared long before us, about 140 million years ago, while dinosaurs still walked the earth. And while there are many creatures in the sea more mighty and just as capable of making lunch of a human being, it is the shark that has always been described as a "killing machine."

The shark is good at what it does. It is a predator, and one of the best (if not *the* best) at that job in the oceans. But it is not a machine—it's an animal. And it's an animal that takes many years to reach adulthood and reproduce.

But with the fury of fear that *Jaws* struck in them, people believed the only good shark was a dead shark. They caught and killed sharks by the hundreds. They didn't want to eat them, or make leather from their skin. They just wanted to extract revenge—revenge for an imaginary wrong.

I'm sure that neither the filmmaker nor the author ever intended their work to result in such terrible actions. But they struck a fear that is deep within the human mind, and which overwhelmed some people so much they lashed out.

Sharks aren't the only animals that have been the object of human loathing. Snakes and spiders are among people's top ten fears. Even animals like crows and ravens have been condemned just because they have black feathers—legends said the gods turned the birds black as punishment. Bats, as already mentioned, are frequent targets of misunderstanding.

Our Western culture is quick to assign labels of "good guy" and "bad guy." And it's hard to remove those labels once they've been stuck on. Without knowing anything about an animal, its biology, or its role in the natural world, people will say they hate it.

Why?

Good and bad are an invention of humans. Nature doesn't have good guys and bad guys. Predators aren't evil—they're just part of nature. Herbivores aren't victims—they're just part of nature.

Before we make up our minds about how we feel about an animal, we need to learn all we can about it. Sometimes that's hard (especially with the so-called "unlovables"). But only by learning about animals—and each other—can we hope to make decisions that will benefit all of us.

Some of the difficulties we are facing in our own backyards, such as the high population of whitetail deer, are results of the actions people took many years before. Surely the early colonists thought they were doing the right thing by wiping out the wolf, the deer's major predator, in the East. But as time has passed and we've learned more, our perspective on their actions has changed. In their time and from their point of view, they did what seemed to be the right thing. But now we know that in the larger scheme of things, it wasn't the best course to follow. The deer bounced back more quickly than their predators did, and now we must make up for the actions of our predecessors.

Other difficulties are the result of actions people are taking today. Coyotes that have gotten used to people because some people are foolish enough to feed them—which will lead to disaster down the line for the coyote and, possibly, for a person. Cats are still taking a toll on songbirds because some people feel that keeping a house cat in the house is cruel, when keeping a pet cat indoors actually protects its health and well being (as one veterinarian told me, "There's no vaccine against cars."). People call their local animal control officers in a snit because they don't like how the beaver dam looks from their back deck, or in a tizzy because they're afraid the raccoon babies in the chimney will give them rabies.

Before you panic about any wild creature, learn the facts. You can call your state's division of fish and wildlife. They're sure to have booklets and pamphlets about any kind of animal you might encounter. Wildlife biologists, although busy people, are always happy to share their knowledge about wild creatures. You can even call the Fund for Animals hotline at (203) 393-1050, or the Humane Society of the United States. Try these people before you call an exterminator; they can help you find a way to solve the problem without having the animal killed just for being in the "wrong place."

Some people think that we should just leave nature alone and not involve ourselves in the lives of other species. That's a nice idea, but an impractical one. We've disrupted habitats. We've wiped out some species, encouraged others, and imported still others. Yes, we've made a right mess of things. But we can't dust off our hands and walk away, saying "Well, now we'll stop meddling. You're on your own, natural world." We can't do that because we are part of the natural world. Even in our houses, sitting in front of the TV, we're still animals, evolved from other animals, who live off other living things. We're part of nature, and we are a very special part of it because we can choose to help our fellow species in ways they can't even imagine.

We can help tiny shorebirds called piping plovers survive by protecting the beaches where they nest. We can bring wolves back to our national parks. We can bring species back from the brink of extinction or push them over it. We can wait for the mother

raccoon to move her youngsters out of the chimney, and then put a cap over the opening so she can't get back in.

It's our choice, and our responsibility.

Wildlife will be with us always. We need to understand it, appreciate it, and be willing to take responsibility for it.

And of course, enjoy its beauty and variety—especially when the animals are right among us.

Further Reading

To learn more, try the following resources.

America's Neighborhood Bats by Merlin D. Tuttle. Austin: University of Texas Press, 1988.

Batman: Exploring the World of Bats by Laurence Pringle. New York: Scribners, 1991.

Borderland: Origins of the American Suburb, 1820–1939 by John R. Stilgoe. New Haven, Conn.: Yale University Press, 1988.

Crabgrass Frontier: The Suburbanization of the United States by Kenneth T. Jackson. New York: Oxford University Press, 1985.

Heart and Blood: Living with Deer in America by Richard Nelson. New York: Viking, 1997.

House of Life: Rachel Carson at Work by Paul Brooks. Boston: Houghton Mifflin, 1989.

Last of the Wild: Vanished and Vanishing Giants of the Animal World by Robert M. McClung. North Haven, Conn.: Linnet Books, 1997.

Lawn: A History of an American Obsession by Virginia Scott Jenkins. Washington, D.C.: Smithsonian Institution Press, 1994.

Lily Pond: Four Years with a Family of Beavers by Hope Ryden. New York: William Morrow and Company, 1989.

Natural History in America by Wayne Hanley. New York: Quadrangle/The New York Times Book Co., 1977.

Once a Wolf: How Wildlife Biologists Fought to Bring Back the Gray Wolf by Stephen R. Swinburne. Boston: Houghton Mifflin, 1999.

Peterson First Guide to Urban Wildlife by Sarah B. Landry. Boston: Houghton Mifflin Co., 1994.

Rabies, Lyme Disease, and Hanta Virus and Other Animal-Borne Human Diseases in the United States and Canada by E. Lendell Cockrum, Tucson, Ariz.: Fisher Books, 1997.

"Unusual Hantavirus Outbreak in Southern Argentina: Person-to-Person Transmission?" by Rachel M. Wells and others. *Emerging Infectious Diseases* (3) 2:171–174.

Urban Naturalist by Steven D. Garber. New York: John Wiley & Sons, 1987.

When Plague Strikes: The Black Death, Smallpox, AIDS by James Cross Giblin. New York: HarperCollins, 1995.

Where Have All the Birds Gone? by John Terborgh. Princeton, N.J.: Princeton University Press, 1989.

Wild Neighbors: The Humane Approach to Living with Wildlife edited by John Hadidian, Guy R. Hodge, and John W. Grandy. Golden, Colo.: Fulcrum Publishing, 1997.

Wildlife in America by Peter Matthiessen. New York: Viking, 1987.

Wildlife Survivors: The Flora and Fauna of Tomorrow by John R. Quinn. Blue Ridge Summit, Penn.: TAB Books, 1994.

Resources

To learn more about the topics covered in this book, you can contact these organizations. Some have posters and other printed materials available upon request, either at no or low cost.

Bat Conservation International
  P.O. Box 162603
  Austin, TX 78716
  (512) 327-9721
  www.batcon.org

Center for Environmental
  Education
  c/o Antioch New England
  40 Avon St.
  Keene, NH 03431
  (603) 355-3251
  www.cee_ane.org

The Centers for Disease
  Control and Prevention
  1600 Clifton Rd.
  Atlanta, GA 20222
  (404) 639-3311
  www.cdc.gov

Cornell Laboratory of Ornithology
  159 Sapsucker Woods Rd.
  Ithaca, NY 14850
  (607) 254-2473
  www.ornith.cornell.edu

The Fund for Animals
  200 W. 57th St.
  New York, NY 10019
  (212) 246-2096

The Humane Society
  of the United States
  2100 L St. NW
  Washington, DC 20037
  (202) 452-1100
  www.hsus.org

Kids for Saving Earth
  Worldwide
  P.O. Box 421118
  Minneapolis, MN 55442
  (612) 559-1234

The National Audubon
  Society
  700 Broadway
  New York, NY 10003
  (212) 979-3000
  www.audubon.org

The National Wildlife
  Federation
  8925 Leesburg Pike
  Vienna, VA 22184
  (703) 790-4000
  www.nwf.org

The Nature Conservancy
  4245 North Fairfax Dr.
  Arlington, VA 22208
  (703) 841-5300
  www.tnc.org

The Peregrine Fund
  5666 W. Flying Hawk Lane
  Boise, ID 83709
  (208) 362-3716
  www.peregrinefund.org

The Raptor Center
  University of Minnesota
  1920 Fitch Ave.
  St. Paul, MN 55108
  (612) 624-8470

Many other specialized organizations, devoted to particular species or geographic regions, are also active in conservation. To find them, try the Conservation Directory, published annually by the National Wildlife Federation. Check your local library for a copy, or you can order one through the NWF website.

Index

115

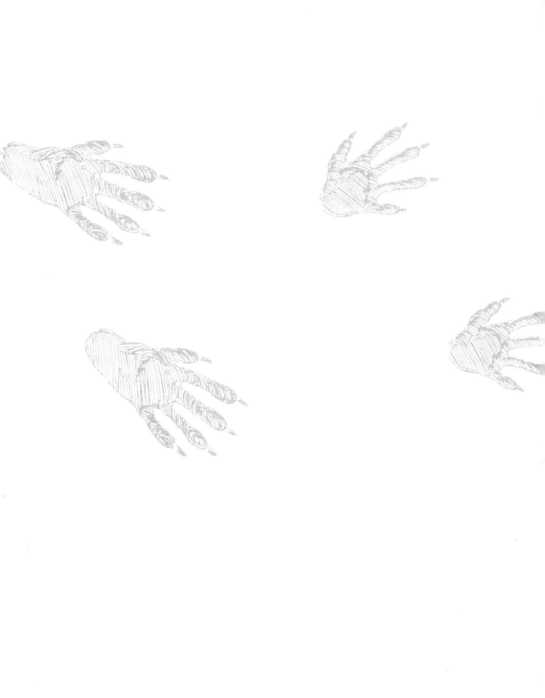